EATING DISORDERS

A TREATMENT WORKBOOK
FOR OUTPATIENTS AND THERAPISTS

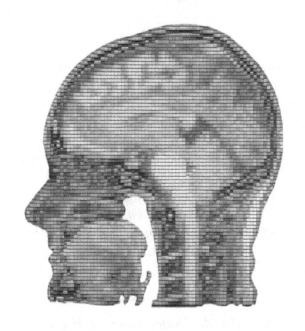

LENORE McKNIGHT, M.D.

Andrew Benzie Books
Walnut Creek, California

Published by Andrew Benzie Books
www.andrewbenziebooks.com

For permission or further information, write to:

Lenore R. McKnight, M.D.
c/o The Williams Firm
1850 MT. Diablo Boulevard, Suite 340
Walnut Creek, CA. 94596

Printed in the United States of America

First Edition: July 2019

ISBN 978-1-941713-82-2

lenoremcknightmd@gmail.com

Edited by Kathleen V. Kish
Cover & book design by Andrew Benzie

*A patient's illness is
not their identity*

Table of Contents

Goals
Expectations
Diet and meal supervision guidelines
Understanding the thoughts/voice of the eating disorder
Therapist and family approach to dealing with anger
Therapist and family approach to meals and snacks
Food rituals and behaviors
Medical management guidelines
How have you hidden your illness from others?
Depression questionnaires
Therapy guidelines
Daily Point Sheet

Goals
Expectations
Reasons why I have my eating disorder questionnaire
Draw a picture of yourself as a person with an eating disorder
Negative thoughts your eating disorder says to you
Thoughts about food worksheet
Digestive system information and quizzes
Time line of your life
Patient's thoughts on eating disorder issues and questionnaire
Family's thoughts on eating disorder issues and questionnaire
Honesty essay

Goals
Expectations
My positive traits and essay
List reasons for your eating disorder, and list positive coping skills
Symptoms and signs of AN (anorexia nervosa) and BN (bulimia nervosa)

Medical complications of eating disorders
Indications for immediate referral for a medical evaluation
Anger questionnaires and essay
Begin to understand your parents
Letter to your family about how your eating disorder has affected them
Confronting your fears essay and questionnaires

Goals
Expectations
Cultural influences on body image
Learning self-acceptance
Body image questionnaires
Steps toward a positive body image
List activities that you are proud of
Write an essay about how you will practice self-acceptance
Responsibility for the path your life takes
List recovery goals
Dealing with the triggers to binge eat, restrict, or purge
Lessons learned from family and friends' questionnaires

Goals
Expectations
Factors of recovery questionnaire
How do you want family and friends to help you?
List activities that you look forward to doing
Draw a picture of your body as you feel about it today
Learn the value of Intuition
Write a letter saying goodbye to your eating disorder
Perseverance essay
Your advice to other patients with an eating disorder
What is recovery?
Signs of relapse
Discharge

Bibliography

About the Author

Chapter One:
Understanding Eating Disorders

Anorexia Nervosa (AN) occurs in about 0.4% of females in their teens and early adulthood. Bulimia Nervosa (BN) occurs in about 1%-1.5% of adolescent and adult females. With both anorexia nervosa and bulimia nervosa the ratio of female to male is about ten to one. These percentages are noted in the DSM-5 for the 12-month prevalence of these illnesses. (DSM-5)

Many factors can produce eating disorders. Genetics can play a large part in both anorexia nervosa and bulimia nervosa, as often the parent or a close relative of a patient will have an eating disorder. Genetic factors may predispose some people to be anxious, obsessive-compulsive, harm avoidant, inhibited, and perfectionistic, characteristics often found in patients with an eating disorder. Research into the neurocircuit function of patients with anorexia nervosa suggests there may be an altered reward modulation in the brains of these patients, so that eating triggers a negative response. (Kaye et al., 2009) Family issues are often a factor in eating disorders. A patient may see their parent diet or make negative comments about their own body. A mother may try to limit her child's food choices or amount of food. Sometimes a relative makes a negative comment about a patient's weight or shape at a family gathering. Some families are overprotective, rigid, or emotionally cold. Other families are chaotic, causing a patient to feel abandoned, misunderstood, and alone. Some patients may find school or work overwhelming. Issues of control are prominent in many patients with eating disorders. Patients who feel unable to control what is happening in their lives may find that the one thing that they can control is their eating. Social factors play a major role in eating disorders. Stressful events, such as relationship issues, can cause a person to restrict their food intake, have binge-eating episodes, or to purge. Patients may be teased about their weight or looks. Movies, television, and magazines often feature thin actresses and models as glamorous and sexy—the "in" woman.

The most common trigger for anorexia nervosa is dieting. If a person has one or several of the above factors or stressors, they may begin to lose weight. At a particular weight—which is different for each person—the gene or genes become triggered if the person is genetically predisposed. Once the gene(s) are triggered, the person develops the illness of anorexia nervosa.

A person with the illness of anorexia nervosa voluntarily restricts their energy (food) intake, which results in an abnormally low body weight. Their extreme fear of gaining weight which could result in their becoming fat prevents them from being able to gain weight. They have a distorted body image, where they see themselves as fat even though they are very thin. Their self-evaluation is based on their perceived body size. They are unable to see the seriousness of their illness.

These patients have strong negative thoughts. They may hear a voice telling them to restrict food, or to lose just five pounds more. They exhibit food behaviors that include skipping meals, eating tiny portions, refusing to eat in front of others, restricting fats, constantly reading food labels, and eating in ritualistic ways. They will give numerous excuses for why they are not eating. They have an obsession with clothing size. They frequently do body checking, which involves pinching or touching their body to see if they are getting fat. When they look in the mirror, they find something to criticize. They need to be thin to feel good about themselves. They see the world as black and white, good or bad. They have rigid and perfectionistic standards for themselves, and can feel they must punish themselves if they do not meet these standards. They often feel anxious. Some exercise to excess. They deny their feelings, especially anger. Starvation makes them become moody and irritable. They feel cold, fatigued, and constipated. They feel that they do not fit in with friends and begin to withdraw from social activities, which usually involve eating and drinking. Many of their relationships become superficial or dependent.

There are two subtypes of anorexia nervosa: restricting type and binge-eating/purging type. People with the restricting type accomplish a low weight by restricting food intake, fasting, or too much exercising. People with the binge-eating/purging type will achieve a low weight by binge eating, then purging by self-induced vomiting or using laxatives, diuretics, or enemas. Patients who purge after eating just small amounts of food are given the binge-eating/purging subtype diagnosis. In both types of anorexia nervosa, patients are fearful of gaining weight and have a distorted body image. The goal of their behaviors is to lose weight and become "thin." Over time, some patients with anorexia nervosa: restricting type move into the diagnosis of anorexia nervosa: binge-eating/purging type.

One study compared 58 adolescent inpatients with one of two different subtypes of AN: 34 patients were diagnosed with the anorexia nervosa/restricting type (AN/R) and 24 patients were diagnosed with the anorexia nervosa/binge-eating/purging type (AN/BEP). This study noted that anxiety was prevalent in both types, being present in 61.8% of the patients with AN/R and in 100% of the patients with AN/BEP. Depression was also very common, being present in 70.6% of the patients with AN/R and in 88.5% of the patients with AN/BEP. Major differences between the two subtypes were found in three other areas: self-mutilation, a history of suicidal behaviors, and substance abuse. A history of self-mutilation was present in 11.8% of the patients with AN/R and in 54.2% of the patients with AN/BEP. A history of suicidal behaviors was present in 2.9% of the patients with AN/R and 33% of the patients with AN/BEP. Finally, a history of substance abuse was present in 14.7% of the patients diagnosed with AN/R and in 41.7% of those patients diagnosed with AN/BEP. (Norton, 2000)

The course and outcomes of anorexia nervosa (AN) are highly variable. Some patients have just one episode, while others have a chronic, unremitting course over many years. Young patients who receive treatment early in their AN illness often have a better long term outcome for their illness. Many patients exhibit a fluctuating course of recovery and relapse. One follow-up paper (Steinhausen, 2002), reviewed a large number of studies of patients with AN who had been hospitalized or who received comprehensive outpatient care and were at least four years beyond the onset of their illness. Good outcome occurred in 46% of the patients with weight restored to within 15% of recommended weight for height and regular menstruation established. Partial recovery was achieved by about 30% of the patients who continued to have residual features of AN. (Steinhausen, 2002) However, even some patients with good recovery and many patients with partial recovery continued to show signs of social phobia, obsessive-compulsive behavior, anorexic thinking (distorted body image), and eating disorder behaviors (avoiding fats). Approximately twenty percent of the patients studied were well below their recommended weight, with menstruation absent. These patients frequently experience multiple medical problems, and the increased possibility of death. Treatment for anorexia can last from two to five years or more.

There have been two recent studies that involve twenty years or more long-term outcome for anorexia nervosa. One study (Eddy et al., 2017), followed participants seeking treatment for AN, and included both inpatients and outpatients. Eddy's criteria for recovery was that the participant was 95% of expected body weight and no binge-eating or purging behaviors, but he allowed for the presence of cognitive features, such as fat phobia, body image disturbance, or overvaluation of weight/shape. Eddy's study reported a recovery rate for participants with AN as 62.8% at a mean of 22 years follow-up. Another study (Fichter et al., 2017) had a long-term follow-up study of over one thousand inpatients with AN. A subsample of 112 patients had a follow-up at a mean of 20 years. Fichter had a stricter definition of remission in that the presence of cognitive symptoms was not allowed. Fichter's study showed a 39.3% remission from AN at 20 years. Fichter noted in his article that if his study had allowed the presence of cognitive symptoms in participants with AN (as in the Eddy's study), the remission rate for Fichter's participants would have been 55.4% at a mean of 20 years. It is difficult to compare studies, for many reasons. For example, Fichter's study may have had sicker patients because they were inpatients.

Bulimia nervosa (BN) is characterized by episodes of binge eating where a person will eat excessive amounts of food within a two-hour time period and feel out of control with this pattern of eating. They are obsessed with their body shape and weight, and they are fearful of gaining weight because of their binge eating. They will try inappropriate compensatory behaviors to prevent weight gain or to lose weight, usually by self-induced vomiting. Patients may also severely restrict their food intake, exercise to the extreme, or misuse medications such as laxatives, diuretics, or diet pills. To be classified as cases of bulimia nervosa, such inappropriate compensatory behaviors must occur at least one time a week for a period of three months. Serious physical and psychological problems can result: chest pains, constipation, abdominal bloating, and life-threatening esophageal tears from excessive vomiting.

Bulimia nervosa is an illness that involves obsessions with food and fear of gaining weight. Patients with this illness may be of normal weight or a person with a larger body. They may sneak into the kitchen at night and binge eat any food in the cupboards or refrigerator. They may steal food from stores because they cannot afford to buy the amount of food needed for their frequent binge-eating/purging episodes, which could involve eating 5,000 calories or more at a time. They partake of such binge foods as ice cream, chips, and pizza. They sometimes vomit in cans and bags hidden in their rooms. They can vomit so much that they plug the toilet or shower drain. These binge-eating/purging episodes can occur from once a week, to after every meal, to five times or more in a day. After a binge-eating/ purging episode, the person may say initially that they feel calm or even "high" because they have purged out all their negative feelings. This is followed by shame and self-loathing and feeling helpless to stop these behaviors. They can have feelings of anxiety, guilt, depression, and hopelessness. They can have problems with substance abuse, impulsivity, suicidal actions, and self-mutilation, which is often related to sexual abuse. There is a correlation as high as fifty percent between a person who does self-mutilation and their having a history of sexual abuse.

One follow-up study of women with bulimia nervosa found that 74% of the women had full recovery, and 99% had partial recovery by the end of the 7.5 year study. Approximately one third of the women relapsed after full recovery (Herzog 1999). Treatment can last from six months to two years or more. Patients with bulimia nervosa often have co-morbid conditions, such as anxiety, depression, post traumatic stress disorder, or bi-polars illness.

Chapter Two:
Eating Disorder Workbook Information

This workbook is designed to provide a cohesive treatment framework for adolescent and adult outpatient eating disorder treatment programs, such as a partial hospitalization programs (PHP), intensive outpatient programs (IOP), and individual outpatient therapy. This workbook allows the program or the therapist to use the type of therapies that they think would be most helpful for their patients or clients. In some programs and in individual outpatient therapy, the patient is referred to as a client. **In this workbook, the word, "family" includes, but is not limited to, individuals that are usually part of the household, such as parents, spouses, partners, grandparents, siblings, and good friends.**

This workbook offers guidelines for meal monitoring, essay topics, questionnaires, and worksheets. The workbook is organized using stages of treatment to help keep the treatment team coordinated with the patient's treatment goals. By having intensive therapy, getting healthy, and engaging with the workbook, the patient will begin to understand the medical complications of their illness and explore body image issues. The patient will start to be honest with themselves and others, to understand their anger, and to confront their fears, They gain self-acceptance and self-esteem. They come to realize that their illness is not their identity.

Most eating disorder treatments are highly structured, which most patients find helpful in their recovery. Patients receive medical monitoring, psychiatric evaluation, and intensive therapy involving many different modalities of treatment, which may include process groups, yoga and relaxation therapy, anger management, assertivesness groups, art and dance therapy, drug and alcohol education, cognitive behavior therapy (CBT), dialectic behavior therapy (DBT), mindfulness, individual therapy, and family therapy.

This workbook has five stages: Stage One (Safety), Stage Two (Awareness), Stage Three (Participation), Stage Four (Action), and Stage Five (Discharge). The written material, questionnaires, and worksheets are easier in the earlier stages because many entry-level patients are so malnourished that they have difficulty thinking. As patients get healthier, their questionnaires and worksheets are more difficult, and the written material more abstract.

Stage One (Safety): The patient begins the refeeding process and learns the guidelines for meals and snacks, medical monitoring, exercise, therapy, and the Daily Point Sheet. Eating food and gaining weight is the essential step in helping patients with anorexia nervosa make progress toward recovery. The therapists and family use the same guidelines to monitor meals and snacks, and they also receive guidelines on how to deal with the patient. Therapist and family must not beg, threaten, shame, criticize, or get angry at a patient. The therapists and family must learn the three Cs—stay calm, caring, and consistent.

Stage Two (Awareness): The patient is eating 100% of their meals with some liquid supplementation, if needed. A patient with BN is not purging. The patient studies the digestive system. They learn more about the underlying reasons for their illness. The patients learn about honesty. By being honest with themselves and others about their eating disorder thoughts and actions, the patients are confronting the eating disorder, which takes away its power of secrecy.

Family involvement is very important to the treatment of patients with eating disorders, and family therapy sessions are regularly scheduled. There are several worksheets that help the patient and therapists to understand some of the underlying dynamics of the family.

Stage Three (Participation): The patient is eating their meals within the time limit with no liquid supplement. Patients begin to have meal outings with family. Patients learn about the medical complications of eating disorders. They list their inner positive traits, such as friendliness, caring, intelligence, and athleticism. These words defined the person before they lost their identity to their eating disorder illness. Patients begin to understand their anger and the concept of forgiveness. The patients are beginning to separate themselves from their illness. Many patients with eating disorders are fearfull of uncertainty, so they try to control everything. Patients must learn to confront their fears of uncertainty and other fears with courage and a belief that they can learn from life's experiences, good and bad.

Stage Four (Action): The patients are eating 100% of their meals and eating some of their taboo foods. They have had successful meal outings with family or friends, and they have experiences better relationships with family and friends.

Patients are learning about cultural influences on body image. They are learning how to have self-acceptance of their bodies and of themselves and to become more assertive. They are accepting some responsibility for the path their life takes. Most importantly, they are learning coping skills to deal with triggers in their life that would make them want to restrict, have binge-eating episodes, and to purge.

Stage Five (Discharge): The patient works on commitment to recovery and relapse prevention. They learn the value of using their intuition. The patient writes a letter saying goodbye to their eating disorder. They also write a letter to their family about how they want those people to support them once they are back at home. They will understand the importance of presevering in their recovery. The lists titled "What is Recovery" and "Signs of Relapse" are shared at this level. These lists are very helpful to therapists and patients alike.

Workbook Guidelines

1 Patient will bring the workbook every day to the program, or to the therapy session.

2 The workbook has five Stages. The patient starts at Stage One and will move through the stages to Stage Five. At each stage there are goals and expectations that need to be met in order to move to the next stage.

3 Each stage has written material that the patient is to read and quizzes, drawings, essays, and questionnaires that must be completed.

4 A patient can be considered for the next stage by the treatment team when the patient has shown good progress with the goals and expectations of the current stage, and the patient's workbook material has been reviewed and signed off by the therapist, the physician(MD), and the registered dietitian(RD). This plan helps keep the treatment team coordinated with the patient's treatment goals.

5 In the more intensive programs, the decision to change a patient's stage is often made during a treatment team meeting.

6 Blank pages in this workbook can be use for assignments that are given to the patient.

7 A therapist may want to add to this workbook's goals and expectations. The therapist may add any other goals and/or expectations that they think are important for their patient's therapy.

8 Some patients benefit from daily feedback about their progress.

9 This workbook offers a Daily Points Sheet.

Daily Points Sheet guidelines

1   A patient will be given points for participating in groups, program activities, finishing workbook assignments, and their behavior during meals and snacks (e.g., finishing meals, decreasing eating disorder behaviors.)

2   The number of points a patient can earn in a day depends on the daily length of the program. Some programs are all day, and some are part of a day. Individual therapists see the patient for one hour, one or more times a week.

3   At home, a family member may be responsible for filling out the part of the daily points sheet concerning meals and snacks.

4   The daily points sheet will be carried from activity to activity during the day by the patient who will get the therapist/MD/RD/RN/family to evaluate each activity.

5   A patient will also set a daily goal each time they come to the program or go to the therapist. This goal will be listed at the top of the daily points sheet.

6   The daily points sheet is turned in at the end of each program day or each therapy session.

7   A patient can be considered for the next stage by the treatment team when the patient obtains a set number of daily points for a set number of days (determined by the program or therapist).

8   Some programs or therapists may choose to use the Daily Point Sheet on a weekly basis. If a patient has accrued a certain number of points by the end of the week, the patient will receive a reward or privilege.

*Note: The reader of this book has this author's permission to copy the Daily Points Sheet or it can be downloaded from: www.andrewbenziebooks.com/dailypointssheet.pdf

**Note: A program or therapist may choose to not use the daily points system. The alternative is the patient can be considered for the next stage by the treatment team when the patient has shown good progress with the goals and expectations of the current stage, and the patient's workbook material has been reviewed and signed off on by the therapist, the physician(MD), and the registered dietitian(RD).

DAILY POINTS SHEET   DATE:

Daily Goal: _____

Circle appropriate number for each activity, add up each column, sum to get total points earned each day. Physician/RD/RN/therapist/family to fill out sheet after each activity.

Vitals	0 (same or worse)	1 (better)	2 (Normal)
Breakfast	0 (didn't eat, ED behaviors)	1 (needed supplement, some ED behaviors)	2 (ate 100%, no ED behaviors)
Check in give goals	0 (didn't come and/or talk, struggled to give goals)	1 (talked some, concrete goals)	2 (active participation, abstract goals)
Workbook	0 (didn't bring)	1 (brought workbook, tried to do assignments)	2 (brought workbook, did assignments)
AM snack	0 (didn't eat or drink)	1 (needed supplement)	2 (ate snack)
Process group	0 (didn't come and/or talk, much denial, no insight)	1 (talked some, some insight, some denial)	2 (Insightful, leadership in group),
Specialty group	0 (didn't come, or participate)	1 (participated)	2 (Insightful, active participation)
Lunch	0 (didn't eat, ED behaviors)	1 (needed supplement, some ED behaviors)	2 (ate 100%, no ED behaviors)
Body image group	0 (hates body, much body checking)	1 (considering self-acceptance)	2 (practicing self acceptance)
PM snack	0 (didn't eat or drink)	1 (needed supplement)	2 (ate snack)
Specialty group	0 (didn't come, or participate)	1 (participated)	2 (insightful, active participation)
Dinner	0 (didn't eat, ED behaviors)	1 (needed supplement, some ED behaviors)	2 (ate 100%, no ED behaviors)
HS snack	0 (didn't eat or drink)	1 (needed supplement)	2 (ate snack)
Column total	____	____	____

Total: _____

Specialty Groups may include: individual therapy, nutrition, family therapy, yoga, mindfulness, art, drama, dance, CBT, DBT, movement, CD, outings, relapse prevention, equine therapy, psychodynamic therapy, assertiveness, multi-family groups, meal outings, recovery goals.

Chapter Three:
Eating Disorder Questionnaire

How often do you agree with each statement?

1 = Never   2 = Sometimes   3 = Frequently   4 = Always

1   I would like to be thinner ____
2   I have been teased about my weight ____
3   I read labels on foods to monitor calories and fat content ____
4   I have tried diet pills and laxatives ____
5   I feel bad about my lying ____
6   I am frequently constipated ____
7   I exercise more than one hour per day ____
8   I use shame to control myself and others ____
9   I have difficulty sleeping ____
10   I set very high standards for myself ____
11   I do not think my boss is ever satisfied ____
12   I have suffered sexual abuse ____
13   I feel overwhelmed by my schoolwork ____
14   I do not feel hungry when I am depressed ____
15   I have difficulty expressing my feelings ____
16   I think my work is very stressful ____
17   I think my mother is controlling ____
18   I think my home is chaotic ____
19   I look at eating disorder websites ____
20   I cook meals for others, but I do not eat the meal ____

21 I think I have too much responsibility in my household ____
22 I have low self-esteem ____
23 I have secrets in my life ____
24 I have cut or burned myself ____
25 I worry about growing up and leaving home ____
26 I refuse meals with friends by saying, "I just ate" ____
27 I binge eat and purge ____
28 I purge after eating even small amounts of food ____
29 I feel addicted to purging ____
30 I must keep my weight under 100 pounds ____
31 I purge to deal with my feelings ____
32 I cannot deal with my alcoholic husband ____
33 I have difficulty dealing with loss ____
34 I am a perfectionist ____
35 I have extreme mood swings ____
36 I feel guilty if I do not exercise after eating ____
37 I feel out of control with my eating disorder ____
38 I do not like to eat in front of people ____
39 I try to avoid conflict ____
40 I feel that my eating disorder is my best friend ____
41 I feel safe in my world of food and weight ____
42 I feel a sense of power when I am able to refuse food ____
43 I have binge-eating episodes when I am stressed ____
44 I want my father's approval, but he never seems to give it ____
45 I lie to my therapist about how much I have eaten ____
46 I weigh my self more than once a day ____
47 I hope to die from my eating disorder ____
48 I have fainted ____
49 I have stolen food or laxatives ____
50 I have difficulty with intimacy ____
51 I am always anxious ____
52 I have many food rituals ____
53 I wear baggy clothes to conceal my weight ____
54 I would like to lose five more pounds ____
55 I do not think I need treatment ____

Chapter Four:
Stage One (Safety)

Stage One (Safety) goals

Sign safety contract on initial interview

Sign program treatment contract

Learn and comply with program rules and guidelines

Begin refeeding process

Begin outpatient eating disorders workbook

Learn about depression

Begin family therapy

Understand and comply with daily points sheet

Stage One (Safety) expectations

Nutritional Expectations

Read and follow guidelines for meal monitoring

Read the advice to parents and therapists concerning meal monitoring

Meet with the registered dietitian (RD) to get menu plan

Attempt to eat, or drink, all meals and snacks

Become aware of your eating disorder rituals

Family to cook and pack all meals and snacks for program, school, or work, and supervise all meals at home

Family may be responsible for filling out the part of the daily points sheet concerning meals and snacks when patient is eating at home

List food rituals and obsessive-compulsive behaviors

Medical Expectations

Read and follow medical management guidelines

Cooperate with weights and vitals, (e.g., if weighed with clothes on, no weights in pockets)

If you are a patient with anorexia nervosa (AN), work to get/maintain medical stability

If you are a patient with bulimia nervosa (BN), work on having no binge-eating episodes and no purging behaviors (purging behaviors includes self-induced vomiting, fasting, excessive exercise, and misuse of diuretics, laxatives, and other medications)

No exercise, either in the program or outside of the program

Limit subtle forms of exercise (e.g. constantly standing, or moving legs when sitting)

Complete all lab requisitions, urine samples, and medical appointments

Physician, usually a psychiatrist, to evaluate patient for possible need of medication for BN, or co-morbid illnesses.

Therapy Expectations

List three goals for this stage and ways you plan to achieve these goals

Read and follow program or therapist's rules

Attend all groups and/or therapy sessions; may need prompting

Bring workbook/assignments to program or therapy sessions; may need prompting

List activities that you have missed or friends and family that you have lost because of your eating disorder(ED)

Begin to confront your denial of your illness

List Ways that you have hidden your illness from others

Begin family therapy

Answer Depression questionnaires

Make sure daily points sheet filled out and turned in to program or to therapist at end of day

Restrictions

Full observation

Watched when going to bathroom

No exercise

If patient is unable to eat or drink their meal plans, is losing weight, becomes medically unstable, persists in exercising, or having binge-eating/purging behaviors, or physically becomes a danger to themselves or others, they may be referred to a more intensive level of treatment, such as inpatient medical hospitalization, inpatient psychiatric hospitalization, or residential treatment

List your goals for Stage One and ways that you plan to achieve these goals

Example: Purge less

    a Distract myself by playing cards

    b Breathe through the tough times

    c Ask staff to help me

1

    a

    b

    c

2

    a

    b

    c

3

    a

    b

    c

Diet and meal supervision guidelines

Before meals

1   A registered dietitian (RD) will provide a nutritional assessment to establish the initial calorie level of a patient's meal plan.
2   The registered dietitian will increase calories as needed to promote steady weight gain for patients with anorexia nervosa.
3   The registered dietitian will plan three meals per day and two to three snacks per day.
4   The registered dietitian will meet with the patient to work on menus, to decrease distorted beliefs about eating, and to increase healthy, realistic beliefs about food and weight.
5   Some registered dietitians will not allow a patient to be a vegetarian, unless the patient was a vegetarian prior to the start of their eating disorder.
6   Patient is to eat what is prepared by the family or program staff, as recommended by the registered dietitian.
7   Program staff decides where a patient will sit at the table for the meals and snacks.
8   A patient will wear a short sleeve shirt during meals to prevent the hiding of food.
9   If a patient is late for a designated meal time, they will not be given extra time to eat.

During meals

1   No trading or negotiating items on the prepared food.
2   Patients will not be given extra soy sauce, mustard, vinegar, or other salty condiments that could result in water retention.
3   No caffeine or diet food or drinks are allowed unless ordered by the registered dietitian.
4   Patients will be observed 100% of the time while eating to ensure that all food and drinks prepared are consumed.
5   All meals must be eaten within 30 minutes and snacks within 15 minutes.
6   If a patient does not finish 100% of a meal, but has eaten more than 50% of a meal, they must drink one liquid supplement, such as Ensure Plus, or equivalent nutritional supplement. If less than 50% of a meal is consumed, two liquid supplements must be consumed. Fifty percent means at least half of every part of the meal is consumed—meat, vegetables, fruit, milk, nuts, and dessert. Liquid supplements must be consumed within five minutes.
7   The following eating disorder behaviors will result in a patient being given one liquid supplement because such behaviors result in the patient having eaten less than 100% of the meal:
    a   Having food "accidentally" hit the floor.
    b   Passing food to peers.
    c   Hiding food in clothing.
    d   Hiding food on the tray or under plates and cups.
    e   Wiping food onto skin or clothes (e.g., butter, mayonnaise).
    f   Spitting food into napkins.

8 Patients will not talk about food or food rituals during mealtime; they must reserve these topics for discussion with RD, MD, or therapist.

9 Patients may not get up from the table during meals (e.g., to throw something away, use the bathroom, change seats, make phone calls).

10 Patients may not eat more than what is on their menu plan without permission from the registered dietitian, therapist, or family.

11 If a patient refuses a meal and/or liquid supplement, a consequence will be given, such as bed rest at home to conserve calories. The patient is not allowed to go to school or work.

12 If a patient refuses to eat, they may be referred to a medical hospital to keep their medical condition stable.

After meals

1 A patient must show therapist, registered dietitian, or family their plates, cartons, or containers to show they drank or ate all the prepared food.

2 Patients will be monitored (line of sight) for one hour after meals and 30 minutes after snacks while in a program, at home, with a therapist, or at school (if possible).

3 Patients may be asked to fill out a "Thoughts about Food" worksheet after breakfast, lunch, and dinner for review with the registered dietitian or therapist. This worksheet is on a single sheet of paper folded in halves, with one side labeled Distorted Thought, such as, "This is too much food." The other half of the paper is labeled Healthy Thought, such as, "This is an appropriate amount of food. It will not make me fat."

4 If a patient purges a meal, they will be given two liquid supplements. If a patient purges a snack, they will be given one liquid supplement.

5 A patient may not use the bathroom for one hour after a meal or snack. If a patient must use the bathroom, the following rules will apply:

    a The patient must be accompanied by therapist or family.

    b The patient may not fully close the bathroom door; however, privacy will be respected.

    c Patient may be asked to talk or sing while in the bathroom.

    d Therapist or family will check the toilet and bathroom before the patient is allowed to flush the toilet or wash their hands.

    e The patient will be monitored for excessive use of toilet paper, which can be used to cover vomit.

6 A patient will not be allowed to move to a higher stage if they attempt to trade or negotiate items on the meal tray.

7 A patient cannot move to a higher stage until they are attempting to eat in a less eating disorder manner. They must work toward eliminating the following rituals:

    a Organizing food on the plate.

    b Cutting food, such as apples, bananas, melons, and pineapple into very small pieces.

c Peeling grapes and eating small bites at a time.

d Pulling apart sandwiches with their fingers.

e Eating foods in a certain order.

f Using silverware to eat apples, bananas, and sandwiches.

g Separating different foods on the plate so that they do not touch each other.

h Not letting lips touch silverware.

i Comparing one's meal tray with a peer's tray.

j Moving food around the plate to make it look as if the food has been eaten.

k Chewing food a set number of times before swallowing.

m Mixing foods together inappropriately.

n Eating slowly and then rapidly finishing the meal just before the end of meal or snack time limit.

o Cutting the crust off bread.

Information for therapist and family

Therapist and family need to understand the illnesses called anorexia nervosa and bulimia nervosa. Patients are controlled by an eating disorder voice that tells them destructive lies: *You are fat. You are ugly. Food equals fat and pounds. Food will make you become huge. You are a burden to take care of. You are never going to accomplish anything in your life. You are pathetic and weak. You do not deserve to live.*

Eating disorder voices or thoughts make patients anxious about eating and fearful of gaining weight. The voices are so disruptive that patients are unable to focus on daily life. The eating disorder has so overtaken their thoughts and actions that the illness has become their life. They focus on nothing but food, weight, and looks. Patients pull back from their friends and family. Patients are reduced to restricting food or binge eating/purging as their only way of dealing with trauma and all of their feelings. They feel safe in their eating disorder world.

When a therapist or family member ask a patient with an eating disorder to eat, that patient feels more afraid of the eating disorder voice in their head than of the voice of the person speaking to them. The eating disorder voice sounds so compelling when telling a patient that food will make them fat that this voice causes the patient to restrict their diet in a variety of ways.

Patients with bulimia nervosa may be willing to eat meals and snacks, sometimes even trying to steal extra food from peers in order to binge eat. After eating, they will have fears of gaining weight and will become intensely preoccupied with trying to purge. These patients need to be closely watched during meals to make sure that they are not spitting food into napkins, and after meals they should be restricted from access to bathrooms and to containers into which they could purge. After purging, they frequently have guilt and self-loathing. Patients with bulimia nervosa experience strong negative eating disorder thoughts and cannot stop thinking about weight and binge-eating/purging behaviors even though their bodies are being destroyed by their purging behaviors.

Patients with eating disorders often have a strong need to be in complete control. This extends to every aspect of their lives, including what they eat. Patients have been known to say that they were trying so hard to be in control that they were out of control.

Therapist and family approach to dealing with anger

It is important for therapist and family to question, understand, and monitor their anger.

Examples

Am I angry because a patient refuses to eat, hides food, or regularly purges?

Am I responding in a negative manner when a patient becomes hostile?

Do I feel incompetent because a patient is not getting better?

Is a patient embarrassing me because they are hiding food while under my watch?

Do I think a patient is being selfish or just wants attention?

Is a patient triggering my own issues around food and weight?

Do I feel guilty as a parent because my child has this illness?

As a parent, am I expressing my feelings through anger?

Do I think that a patient is projecting (putting) their anger onto me?

To treat a patient with an eating disorder, remember the three C's: Calm, Caring, and Consistent. Stay calm and do not show anger. Stay caring and do not criticize, threaten, or beg. Stay consistent with the rules.

By remembering the three C's, therapist and parents are able to gain a patient's trust and help them to move beyond their illness. Therapist and family should project a sense of hope for recovery.

Therapist and family approach to meals and snacks

1 Be firm and consistent but compassionate. If therapist or family are not consistent with the rules of supervision, a patient can feel unsafe with eating.

2 Do not allow negotiation. The registered dietitian creates a meal plan to ensure that a patient has received a balanced and nutritious meal. If a patient has concerns about their menu plan, the registered dietitian can be consulted.

3 Let a patient know that food is their medicine.

4 Supportive statements could be, "I know you can do this. You deserve to eat. Tell me what you are thinking. I'm here for you. I am concerned about you."

5 Liquid supplements (e.g., Ensure Plus) are not a punishment but an alternative to the food that the patient did not eat.

6 Do not talk about weight, food, calories, body size, or clothing. For patients, these topics are triggers for restricting or wanting to purge.

7 Be aware of personal issues concerning food, calories, and weight; and be careful not to mention these to a patient.

8 Do not make comments to the patient about their appearance. If you say to the patient, *you look good,* their eating disorder thought will be, *I must be getting fat.*

9 If a patient uses the word *fat* in a sentence, it is probably their eating disorder thoughts/voice talking.

10 Encourage a patient to try and confront their eating disorder thoughts/voice.

11 Do not express anger. Do not beg or threaten a patient. Do not criticize or shame.

12 Understand that what seems like resistance to eating is often the result of a patient's eating disorder voice saying: *If you eat that food, you will get fat.* A patient gets a glazed-over look as if listening to an internal voice, and they are unable to respond to encouragement to eat. Do not argue with the eating disorder voice.

13 Resist feeling guilty if a patient does not make positive changes concerning their eating and their eating disorder thoughts.

14 Understand that a person cannot change if they do not want to change. The ultimate responsibility for recovery belongs to the patient.

15 Be honest in what you say. Eating disorders are illnesses of lies and secrecy.

16 Be ready to learn from a patient about how they see themselves.

17 Be sensitive and caring about a patient's fears.

18 Never give up on a patient. They need you to believe in them.

19 Project a sense of hope for recovery.

Food rituals and behaviors

List your food rituals

    1

    2

    3

    4

    5

List your taboo foods

    1

    2

    3

    4

    5

List your obsessive-compulsive behaviors

    1

    2

    3

    4

    5

Medical management guidelines

1   Patients will have their orthostatic vital signs taken while sitting in a chair quietly for five minutes. Vitals will be retaken after the patient has been standing quietly for two minutes.

2   Orthostatic vital signs can be taken once or twice a day, to several times a week, to once a week, depending on the intensity of the program or therapy, and the medical health of the patient.

3   If vital signs are very low and/or unstable, a patient will be sent for a medical evaluation, possibly resulting in an inpatient medical or inpatient psychiatric admission.

4   A patient may take only one 15-minute shower per day, which must be taken in the morning before breakfast. This helps prevent purging.

5   Patients will have their weight taken once or more during a week, depending on the intensity of the program, and the medical condition of the patient.

6   Usually, a patient will be weighed after urinating, while wearing a hospital gown and underware, including bra if female. All other items, including socks and jewelry, must be removed.

7   Patients will be weighed with their backs to the scale. Therapist/RD/MD/RN will usually not tell a patient their weight, unless the treatment team has decided that the patient should know their weight.

8   How much a patient should weigh at time of discharge and their healthy body weight will be set by the patient's eating disorder treatment team. Most patients usually have a physician, a registered dietitian, and a therapist involved in their care.

9   The physician will order blood tests, urine tests, EKGs, and any other tests that are needed. The patient is responsible for following up on these tests when they are ordered.

10   In the program and at home, the bathroom door will be locked for one hour after meals and for 30 minutes after snacks.

11   If a patient is suspected of purging, exercising, or water loading in the bathroom, the bathroom door will be kept locked and only unlocked by therapist or family when necessary.

12   Patients may not do exercise, either in the program or outside of the program, until authorized by the physician(MD).

13   A patient will be observed for subtle forms of exercise, such as constantly standing, excessive pacing, or having feet in motion while sitting.

14   Consequences for exercising during the day, either in or out of the program, may include monitoring (line of sight), more interaction with the therapist or family, not being able to progress to further stages, or being dropped back a stage.

15   Consequences for exercising at night may include monitoring (line of sight).

16   Patients are not allowed to dress in light-layered clothing in an attempt to burn extra calories by shivering.

17   No food, liquids, water bottles, or cups are allowed in a patient's room at home.

18 A patient's room will usually be checked by family each day for hoarding of food or water and for signs of vomit.

19 No current medication is available to stop the eating disorder voice/thoughts.

20 Patients with BN will be evaluated for a medication.

21 Patients will be evaluated for any co-morbid conditions which may benefit from a medication trial, such as depression, OCD, PTSD, anxiety, psychosis, and bi-polar disorder.

List ways that you have hidden your eating disorder illness from others
Example: I wear baggy clothes so people will not notice that I have lost weight

1

2

3

4

5

6

7

8

9

10

Therapy guidelines

1 Patients will attend and participate in all therapy groups.
2 Patients will be encouraged in group and individual therapy to understand the underlying dynamics of their illness and to confront their eating disorder voice.
3 Patients will be given a journal and encouraged to write daily in their journal.
4 Patients will be discouraged from looking at fashion magazines.
5 Patients may have weekly family therapy sessions in which family issues and dynamics will be explored. The family is educated about the illness and how they can help the patient.
6 Patients will meet with a physician for medication evaluation/management.
7 Each program will have their own behavioral guidelines.
8 Each patient will have their own individual treatment plan and will move through the stages at their own pace.

Draw a picture or write about how you feel when you are alone

List activities that you have missed or friends and family that you have lost because of your eating disorder

1

2

3

4

5

6

7

8

9

10

Depression questionnaire

Many patients with an eating disorder suffer from depression. Some patients may have been depressed prior to their eating disorder. Starvation can cause depression. It is helpful for a patient's recovery to understand and treat the reasons for their depression.

Mark x for any statements that apply to you.

_____ I am depressed most of the day.

_____ I do not want to get out of bed in the morning.

_____ I have lost or gained weight recently.

_____ I worry about my grades in school.

_____ I was depressed before my eating disorder.

_____ I always feel tired.

_____ I don't eat when I am depressed.

_____ I have had suicidal thoughts.

_____ I have made a suicidal attempt.

_____ I have a relative that has committed suicide.

_____ I cannot concentrate at work.

_____ I feel worthless.

_____ I am a burden to my family.

_____ I have problems sleeping.

_____ I have recurrent thoughts of death.

_____ I have difficulty making decisions.

_____ I can't imagine a future.

_____ I start to binge eat when I am depressed.

_____ I don't think my friends want to be around me.

_____ I isolate myself by playing games on my iPhone.

_____ I feel restless and agitated.

_____ Sometimes I hear voices in my head.

_____ I wonder if I am "losing my mind."

_____ I have used street drugs and/or alcohol.

_____ I have racing thoughts in my head.

_____ I feel guilty about things that I have done.

_____ I smile even when I am sad because people expect it.

_____ I am not interested in doing my usual activities.

_____ I am angry, mean, and rude to the people closest to me.

_____ I can't get motivated to do anything around the house.

_____ I have taken medication for my depression.

_____ I obsess about past experiences.

_____ I find a dark room comforting.

_____ I cry often.

_____ I have called the suicide hotline (1-800-273-8255).

List times in your life when you were feeling sad or depressed

    1

    2

    3

    4

    5

    6

Name people who have helped or could help you deal with your sadness or depression

    1

    2

    3

    4

When I am lonely, sad or depressed, I will try to use the following coping skills
Example: Write in my journal

    1

    2

    3

    4

    5

    6

*"Every man has his secret sorrows which the world knows not;
and often times we call a man cold when he is only sad."*

Henry Wadsworth Longfellow

STOP

DO NOT CONTINUE UNTIL YOU HAVE THE FOLLOWING SIGNATURES:

THERAPIST _____

DIETITIAN (RD) _____

PHYSICIAN (MD) _____

Chapter Five:
Stage Two (Awareness)

Stage Two (Awareness) goals

Continue to be safe, with no harmful actions to self or others

Understand program rules and follow them

Eat 100% of meals, with some supplementation

Begin to understand reasons for eating disorder

Confront eating disorder thoughts/voice with Thoughts about Food worksheet

Learn about the digestive system

Develop a therapeutic alliance with therapist

Learn the importance of being honest with self and others

Comply with daily points sheet

Stage Two (Awareness) expectations

Nutritional Expectations

Understand and follow meal monitoring rules

Complete 100% of contracted meal plan with supplements, if needed

Attempt to limit eating disorder rituals

Accept staff or family redirection concerning eating disorder behaviors during meal time

Continue to meet with the RD to work on menus, to decrease distorted beliefs, and to increase healthy and realistic beliefs about food and weight

Do Thoughts about Food worksheet after each meal

Family to cook and pack all meals and snacks for program, school, or work, and supervise all meals at home

Family may be responsible for filling out the part of the daily points sheet dealing with meals and snacks when the patient is eating at home.

Read Digestive System information and complete quizzes

Medical Expectations

Complete all requisitions for urine and blood work and for medical appointments

Maintain medical stability (may still have some orthostatic changes)

If a patient with AN, show some weight gain

If a patient with BN, no binge-eating/purging behaviors (includes no vomiting, diuretics, diet pills, or laxative use)

No exercise, either in the program or outside of program

Limit subtle forms of exercise

Therapy Expectations

List three goals for this stage and ways you plan to achieve these goals

Attend all groups and/or therapy sessions; may need some prompting

Bring workbook/assignments to program or therapy sessions; may need some prompting

Work on understanding and controlling the urge to purge, if this is an issue

Begin to accept constructive feedback

Read all the literature and complete all assignments in this section, including:

"reasons why I have my eating disorder" questionnaire

draw a picture of yourself as a person with an eating disorder

list negative thoughts your eating disorder says to you

write about how have you changed over the last year

draw pictures of the best and worst times of your life

Construct timeline of positives and negatives in your life (your therapist may choose to work with you on developing a horizontal timeline of the ups and downs of your life)

Begin to show interest in motivation for recovery

Begin to understand issues with parents

Attend all planned family therapy sessions

Understand the importance of being honest about your eating disorder behaviors

Restrictions

No exercise

Bathroom and community observations are often still under strict observation, but will be based on individual needs

If patient is not making progress in Stage Two, they may be dropped back to Stage One or considered for a more intensive level of care, such as residential or inpatient psychiatric care

Privilages

Family meal with staff or RD, if offered

List your goals for Stage Two and ways that you plan to achieve these goals

1

    a

    b

    c

2

    a

    b

    c

3

    a

    b

    c

"Reasons why I have an eating disorder" questionnaire

Circle the number of any comments to which you can relate

1   I compare myself with everyone, and I always think that they are thinner than me.

2   I keep my feelings pent up inside of me, and then I purge my feelings by throwing up.

3   I began restricting food to lose weight so that my boyfriend would not break up with me.

4   When my husband died, my life became out of control. I began to focus on dieting and exercise.

5   Restricting my food has helped me to deal with my feelings about being molested.

6   The eating disorder is my identity; I do not know who I am without it.

7   I am a perfectionist, and I want a perfect body. I do not like to be average because then I feel like less of a person.

8   I was harassed by my boss at work.

9   I did not want to eat because I did not think I deserved to eat.

10   I have low self-esteem because my mother is too critical of me. When I get mad at my mother, I direct my anger at myself. This anger causes me to stop eating.

11   I was overwhelmed with the college social activities, the dorm food, and the difficult classes.

12   My divorce was very stressful.

13   I felt alone.

14   I just started losing a little weight, and then it became out of control. I just wanted to be thin. I did not realize that I would become so sick. I would never have signed up for this illness if I had known that I would be so sick.

15 When I am angry, I control others by restricting my food intake. This is part of my revenge.

16 I like being sick, but I do not want to die. Being sick keeps the focus of my family on me rather than on the other problems in the family.

17 At school, there is a lot of pressure to look thin.

18 I was so depressed I did not want to eat.

19 I thought gaining weight would make me look unattractive and then the men would leave me alone.

20 I have issues with trust.

21 I wanted to lose some weight. I could not tolerate starving myself, so I would eat and purge.

22 When my friends rejected me, I withdrew and focused on food and exercise.

23 My parents expected me to make good grades, but my advanced classes were too difficult. I felt out of control with my schoolwork.

24 I became depressed because something happened to my best friend.

25 Everyone said I looked "good" when I lost a few pounds, so I kept dieting.

26 Because my mother was so controlling, the one thing in my life that I could control was my eating.

27 I was told to eat healthy, so I cut out sugar and junk food, then meat, and soon I was eating just 600 calories a day.

28 I hated myself when I argued with my parents.

29 A relative called me fat.

30 I thought I could run faster if I weighed just a few pounds less.

Draw a picture of your life as a person with an eating disorder

List negative thoughts that your eating disorder says to you
Example: Your hip bones do not show enough, you are fat

1

2

3

4

5

6

7

8

9

10

Thoughts about food worksheet

Patients with an eating disorder frequently think they are knowledgeable about nutrition; however, they often have distorted beliefs about what constitutes a healthy menu plan. On the left side of the page, the patient is to write down the eating disorder thoughts they had when they were eating a meal. On the right side of the page, the patient is to write down what would be a healthy thought concerning their meal. The patient is beginning to confront their eating disorder thoughts/voice.

Eating disordered thought
"There is too much fat in this meal."

Healthy thought
"I need to eat fats to be healthy."

Breakfast

Lunch

Dinner

Digestive system

The digestive system processes food and gets rid of body waste. Solid food is broken down into basic components that the body can use for energy or building cells. The basic components are:

Water

Water is the most important substance required by the body. Though water provides no calories, it serves several important functions. It helps to regulate body temperature, it carries nutrients and oxygen throughout the body, and it helps eliminate waste products from the body. The average body loses about 10 cups of water per day through the lungs, skin, and kidneys. Because the body's thirst mechanism is poor, it is important to drink water and fluids throughout the day. By the time you feel thirsty, you could already be dehydrated.

Carbohydrates

Carbohydrates derive their name from the fact that they are made of carbon, hydrogen, and oxygen. Carbohydrates are combinations of individual sugar molecules with the simplest sugar being glucose. There are two kinds of carbohydrates: simple carbs, such as milk, honey, and table sugar, which give quick energy; and complex carbs, such as whole grains, beans and sweet potatoes, which give longer lasting energy.

All carbohydrates are broken down into glucose (sugar) before being absorbed into the bloodstream. Once glucose is in the bloodstream, insulin is secreted from the beta cells in the pancreas to facilitate the passage of glucose going into the cells, which decreases the glucose in the blood. Once inside the cell, the glucose is turned into energy via the Krebs cycle so that the muscles have energy for contraction or for rebuilding of cells.

It is very important that the glucose level in the blood remain relatively stable at 70-99 ml/dl. A patient with anorexia nervosa (AN) may not be eating enough food to keep their blood glucose (sugar) normal. This condition of low blood glucose is called (hypoglycemia). When the blood glucose level goes below 70 ml/dl, the brain, which uses only glucose (sugar) as its source of fuel, begins to malfunction causing a person to suffer from dizziness, headache, shakiness, difficulty thinking clearly, difficulty concentrating, seizures, loss of consciousness, and coma. Low blood sugar can be life threatening. High blood sugar can result when there is a failure of the beta cells in the pancreas that causes the blood sugar to rise above 100ml/dl: ultimately, this can create a condition known as diabetes mellitus.

Proteins

All proteins contain carbon, hydrogen, oxygen, and nitrogen. Structural proteins are the body building blocks that make up muscles, organs, hair, and bones. Functional proteins are the enzymes and hormones that control the many thousands of processes in the human body. Functional proteins can act as the body's messengers between cell populations. Insulin and glucagon are functional proteins. Proteins are needed to produce neurotransmitters, such as serotonin.

Proteins are found in animal and plant foods, such as meat, milk, fish, and eggs, beans, and soy. Proteins are made up of amino acids. There are 22 different amino acids that can be combined in many different ways, just like letters of the alphabet can be combined in thousands of ways to make different words. Just as several letters make a word, several amino acids make a protein. Individual amino acids can be stored in muscle tissue. If the body is starved and does not have enough food to supply the glucose (sugar) that it needs, the amino acids in muscle will be diverted from building muscle to creating glucose. This explains why patients with AN lose muscle, including heart and skeletal muscle, when they restrict food.

There are nine essential amino acids that the body needs supplied each day by food. These essential amino acids cannot be synthesized by the human body. One of the nine amino acids is tryptophan, which is a precursor for serotonin. One cause of depression is thought to be related to low levels of serotonin. Beef, pork, lamb, chicken, seafood, fish, milk, cheese, yogurt, eggs and soybeans and soy products supply all nine of the essential amino acids that the body needs. These products are complete proteins. Plant proteins, such grains, dried beans and peas, and nuts do not have all nine of the essential proteins or have very small amount of some of the essential proteins so they are called incomplete proteins.

Fats

Fats are an important source of energy in the body and for the production of certain hormones, like sex hormones. They are also necessary for the absorption of the fat soluble vitamins A,D,E, and K. During digestion, fats are broken down into subunits called fatty acids. There are three main types of fat: saturated, monounsaturated and polyunsaturated. Saturated fats from meat, chicken, cheese, and whole milk are usually solid at room temperature and are the type associated with cardiovascular disease. Monounsaturated fats (from avocado, nuts and olive oil) and polyunsaturated fats (from vegetable sources, walnuts, and fish) are liquid at room temperature and are considered more heart healthy. Omega-3 fats are polyunsaturated fats. Fats are an important part of every cell membrane (the vital exterior of a cell).

Vitamins

The body needs thirteen essential vitamins to function. These vitamins are A,D,E, and K that are fat soluble vitamins, and vitamins C, B6, B12, B1 (thiamin), B2 (riboflavin), niacin, folate, biotin, and pantothenic acid which are water-soluble vitamins. Vitamins are organic compounds that enable the body to carry out the processes of metabolism or tissue growth and repair. The body cannot synthesize these thirteen essential vitamins and must get them from the diet. Vitamins are found in a wide range of foods, including vegetables, milk, meats, fruits, and grains.

A deficiency in a particular vitamin will cause a specific illness. Vitamin A helps vision and a deficiency can cause night blindness. Vitamin A is found in liver, eggs, whole milk, leafy greens, potatoes, and peaches. Vitamin D is essential for strong bones and it helps the body use calcium from the diet. A deficiency can cause muscle weakness, bone pain and rickets. Vitamin D comes from exposure to the sun and from fish, egg yolks, and fortified dairy and grain products. A deficiency in

Vitamin B12 can cause tingling in the feet and hands, extreme fatigue, weakness, irritability and depression. Vitamin B12 is found in eggs, cheese, milk, fish, liver, red meat and fortified tofu.

Minerals

Minerals, like vitamins, are found in food. Minerals and vitamins are called micronutrients because only small amounts are needed in the body. Minerals are inorganic compounds necessary for the proper functioning of all the tissues in the body. Calcium, phosphorus and magnesium are necessary for strong bones. Sodium and potassium help cell membranes function correctly. Chromium helps control blood sugar levels and zinc supports the immune system and nerve function.

Fiber

Fiber is an indigestible form of carbohydrate and is found in whole grains, beans, fruits, and vegetables. It helps in promoting good digestion and reducing constipation.

Match compound with its job

PROTEINS
(milk, meat, fish)

builds strong teeth
and bones

CARBOHYDRATES
(vegetables, fruits,
bread, cereals)

essential part of cell
membrane

FATS
(milk, eggs, meat)

breaks down to amino
acids which build and
repair cells

MINERALS
(calcium and phosphorus)

helps prevent fatigue,
weakness and irritability

WATER

beaks down to glucose
to give energy

VITAMINS
(B12)

promotes digestion and
reduces constipation

FIBER

helps regulate body
temperature

Match compound with its job (answers)

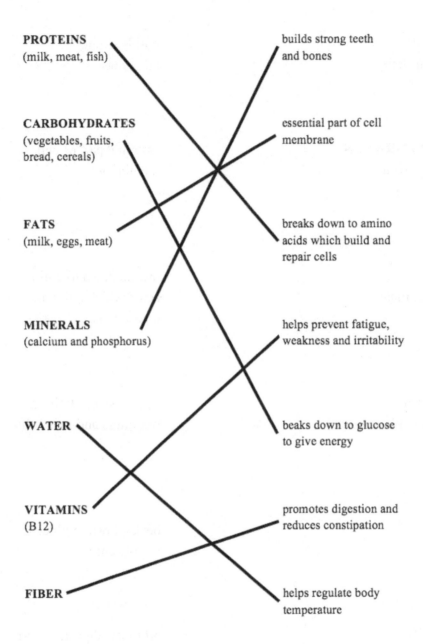

PROTEINS
(milk, meat, fish)

CARBOHYDRATES
(vegetables, fruits,
bread, cereals)

FATS
(milk, eggs, meat)

MINERALS
(calcium and phosphorus)

WATER

VITAMINS
(B12)

FIBER

builds strong teeth
and bones

essential part of cell
membrane

breaks down to amino
acids which build and
repair cells

helps prevent fatigue,
weakness and irritability

beaks down to glucose
to give energy

promotes digestion and
reduces constipation

helps regulate body
temperature

The digestive system

The digestive system is a long tube that goes from the mouth to the anus. Food is mechanically and chemically broken down to its basic components as it goes through the mouth, esophagus, stomach and into the small intestine where food products are absorbed through the small intestinal microvilli. Undigested food passes on to the large intestine where the water is removed and the stool is then passed out of the body through the anus.

Mouth

Our teeth chew up the food and mix the food with saliva which comes from the three salivary glands. The parotid glands are located on both sides of the face at the angle of the jaw and up toward the ear. These glands secrete saliva and produces the enzyme amylase, which breaks carbohydrates into glucose. When you chew a saltine cracker, it will begin to taste sweet because the amylase has changed the cracker starch into glucose (sugar). The submandibular glands are located under the jaw and secrete about 70% of the saliva that is in the oral cavity. The teeth, the tongue, the saliva, and the enzymes form the food into a soft, moist, rounded mass, called a bolus, that can be swallowed.

Esophagus

The esophagus has two layers of muscle, some vertical and some horizontal, that squeeze food down to the stomach in a wave like motion that is called peristalsis. The movement of food down the esophagus to the stomach is very forceful. The esophageal sphincter is a ring of muscle at the junction of the esophagus and stomach. Many people suffer from GERD, gastro-esophageal reflux disease, which means that gastric contents reflux (return) back into the esophagus because the esophagus sphincter did not close tightly or has become weakened over time. There are many causes for this illness, including frequent vomiting, smoking, alcohol, obesity, delayed gastric emptying, and certain medications and foods. Patients with this illness often complain of heart burn (a burning pain just under the breast bone), belching, chronic sore throat, general chest pain, bloating and an acidic taste in the mouth. If there is too much stomach acid in the esophagus ulcers can occur which can lead to precancerous changes in the cells in a condition called Barrett's esophagus.

Stomach

The stomach is located on the left side of the body and is protected by the five lowest ribs. The stomach has muscles going in three different directions so that it can churn the food and mix it with digestive juices. The stomach has the enzyme pepsin that helps digest proteins and carbohydrates. The cells in the stomach wall secrete hydrochloric acid, which helps to kill bacteria in the food. To protect the lining of the stomach from this acid, the stomach has glands that secrete mucus that covers the stomach lining. The food in the stomach becomes a highly acidic semifluid mixture called chyme. At the end of the stomach is the pyloric sphincter which will relax and let small amounts of chyme into the small intestine.

The digestive system

Color the digestive system picture any way you want—expressing feelings you may have about your body.

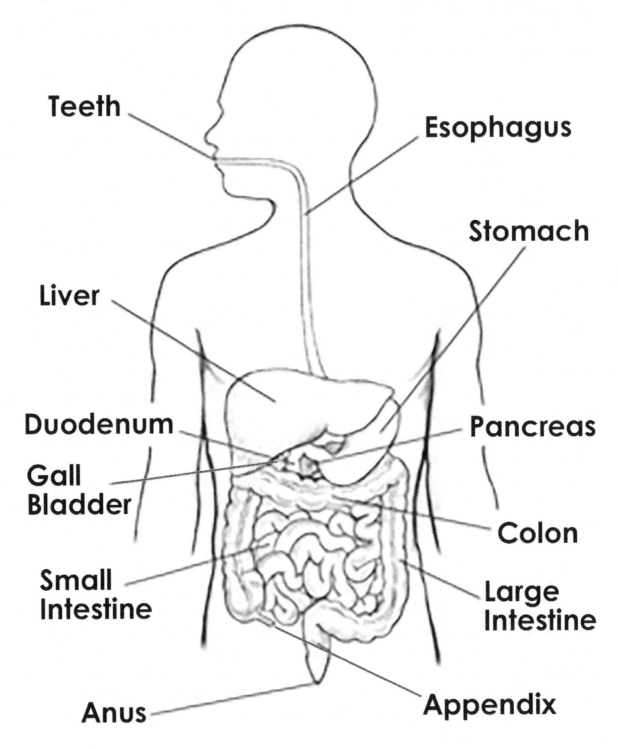

Image courtesy National Institute of Diabetes and Digestive and Kidney Diseases

Small Intestine

The food in the small intestine is broken down into its basic components: glucose, fatty acids, and amino acids. Glucose and amino acids are diffused (absorbed) into the small intestine via the microvilli in the small intestine. The microvilli are fingerlike projections from the surface of the small intestine that are composed of capillaries that absorb amino acids and sugars. Lymph vessels absorb fatty acids. The amino acids, glucose, and fatty acids are transported to the liver via the portal vein. Vitamins, minerals, and water are not broken down in the small intestine, but are absorbed unchanged.

The first part of the small intestine is called the duodenum. Food goes from the stomach through the pyloric sphincter into the duodenum. The food stimulates the mucosal lining of the duodenum to secrete intestinal enzymes and to also release hormones that stimulates digestive enzymes from two major organs; the liver and the pancreas.

Liver

The liver is very involved with fat metabolism. The liver produces a thick, green liquid called bile that is stored in the gallbladder and is transferred to the duodenum via the bile duct. Bile emulsifies fats by breaking larger fat particles into smaller particles which can then be broken into fatty acids by the enzyme lipase. These fatty acids are absorbed (diffused) into the small intestine lymph system and then to the portal vein. From there, some fatty acids go to the muscles and adipose tissue, but most go to the liver where the fatty acids are used to make cholesterol, an essential ingredient in steroid hormones and for nerve cell functioning. Each nerve cell is surrounded by a myelin sheath made up of cholesterol, phospholipids, and protein. The myelin sheath insulates the nerve and enhances the passing of electrical signals in the nervous system. In extreme starvation, the body may use the fat in the myelin sheath for energy. This may explain why some patients have difficulty thinking.

The liver is involved in carbohydrate metabolism. The liver takes the glucose from the blood stream (with the help of insulin) and stores the glucose in the form of glycogen. When the blood level of glucose drops because of fasting or exercise, the liver changes the glycogen to glucose and releases the glucose into the blood stream.

The liver is involved in protein metabolism. The liver takes the amino acids it receives and assembles a new protein that the body needs.

The liver, the largest organ in the body, has more than 500 functions. The liver also stores vitamins, breaks down old blood cells, clears the blood of toxins such as drugs and alcohol, and helps the body resist infections by producing immune factors and removing bacteria from the blood.

Pancreas

The pancreas is a long, thin gland located behind the stomach. The larger end (head) of the pancreas rest in the loop of the duodenum and has a connection to the duodenum via the pancreatic duct. The pancreas secretes into the pancreatic duct four main enzymes: amylase to break down carbohydrates to glucose; lipase to break down fats to fatty acids (with the help of bile from the liver); and trypsin and chymotrypsin, to break down proteins to amino acids.

The pancreas has another major function. Throughout the pancreas are islets of Langerhans, areas of tissue made up mostly of alpha and beta cells. The beta cells release into the blood stream the hormone insulin which regulates the glucose (sugar) level in the blood. When the beta cells stop functioning, the blood glucose level rises (hyperglycemia). When the glucose level in the blood drops (hypoglycemia), the alpha cells release the hormone glucagon into the blood stream. This hormone signals to the liver to break down the stored glycogen to glucose to be released in to the blood stream to maintain a normal level of blood sugar.

Large Intestine

The large intestine absorbs water and any needed electrolytes. Undigested food, like fiber, dead cells shed from the lining of the digestive tract and other waste becomes more solid. This stool is stored in the rectum and until eventually it is pushed out the anus.

Words that relate to the digestive system

In the puzzle below there are eleven hidden words that are related to the digestive system. Draw a circle around each word: appendix, stomach, teeth, liver, protein, pancreas, fats, vitamin, intestine, nutrition, and esophagus.

```
T V A P P E N D I X I R S
E M T C A L R E S P U R T
S N P V R A I U R A O S O
O H A I A I N V W N U V M
P R O T E I N Q E C W J A
H H U A W F Z T D R U T C
A O T M C I S W T E E T H
G T O I C H U X P A D R E
U X Y N W P F A T S L D Z
S N U T R I T I O N T X O
X D I N T E S T I N E P A
```

Words that relate to the digestive system (answers)

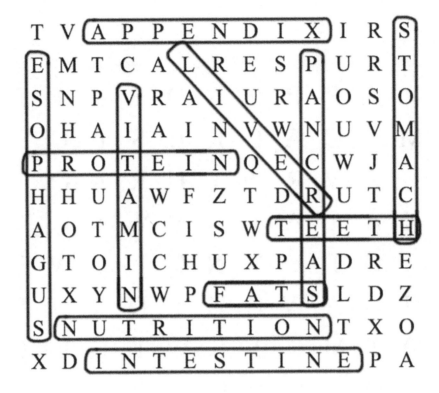

Draw a picture of the happiest time in your life
Now color the picture

How have you changed over this last year?

1

2

3

4

5

Draw or write how you feel about these changes

Time line of your life

Write down the positive and negative events that have happened in your life; e.g. family, school, friends, abuse, illness, work, awards, accidents. You can continue to fill in events as you begin to remember them while in therapy.

Positives		**Negatives**
Example: had pet dog		*Example:* broke wrist
	Age 1-2	
	Age 3-4	
	Age 5	
	Age 6	
	Age 7	
	Age 8	
	Age 9	
	Age 10	
	Age 11	
	Age 12	
	Age 13	
	Age 14	
	Age 15	
	Age 16	
	Age 17	
	Age 18	

Time line as an adult

Positives		**Negatives**
	Age 19-24	
	Age 25-29	
	Age 30-34	
	Age 35-39	
	Age 40-44	
	Age 45-49	
	Age 50-54	
	Age 55-59	
	Age 60-70	

Patient's thoughts on eating disorder issues

Patient's thoughts on:

1 weight

2 dieting

3 fitness

4 perfection

5 control

6 expressing emotions

Patient questionnaire

List your strenghts

    1

    2

    3

    4

    5

List your weaknesses

    1

    2

    3

    4

    5

What issues to you want to talk about in the family meeting?

    1

    2

    3

    4

    5

Family's thoughts on eating disorder issues *(answered by patient)*

Father's thoughts on:

1   Weight

2   Dieting

3   Fitness

4   Perfectionism

5   Expressing emotions

Mother's thoughts on:

1   Weight

2   Dieting

3   Fitness

4   Perfectionism

5   Expressing emotions

Other family member's thoughts on:

1   Weight

2   Dieting

3   Fitness

4   Perfectionism

5   Expressing emotions

Family questionnaire

These questions are to be answered by the father, the mother, and other family members on separate sheets of paper and returned to the therapist.

List your own strengths

List your own weaknesses

List the patient's strengths

List the patient's weaknesses

List what you think you can do to help the patient

How does the patient's eating disorder impact your own life

Issues you want to discuss in a family meeting

List ways you would like your family to treat you
Example: Please don't yell at me

1

2

3

4

5

6

7

8

9

10

Honesty

Honesty is one of the first steps in confronting an eating disorder voice or thoughts. Most patients with an eating disorder are generally honest in their lives; however, their illness makes them lie about how much they eat or how often they purge. By being honest to themselves and to others about their thoughts and actions, patients can take away the power of secrecy that fuels their eating disorder. Honesty is a lesson that everyone must confront—in their actions, words, and thoughts.

Dishonesty of actions can include stealing and cheating.

Example 1: Barbara

Barbara has been purging for two years. She frequently steals food from the grocery store on her way home from work so that she can binge eat and purge in the middle of the night without her family being aware of her behavior.

Example 2: Jason

Jason is getting treatment for anorexia nervosa. He uses a variety of ways to cheat on his meal plan to avoid eating all of his required calories. He will eat half of an apple and slyly hide the other half. He will spit food into a napkin and throw it away. He is fearful of gaining weight and is only able to hear his eating disorder voice.

Dishonesty of words can take many forms.

Example 1: The bold-faced lie

"Janine," asks her father, "did you purge in the bathroom after dinner?" "Oh, no," replies Janine. "Really?" asks her father. "Then why does it smell like vomit in the bathroom?"

Example 2: The little white lie

"Nancy," asks her mother, "did you eat all of your lunch—the sandwich and the fruit? You look like you have been losing weight."
"Yes, Mom, I ate my lunch."
Had Nancy been completely honest, she would have answered: "Yes, I ate lunch, but only the fruit."

Dishonesty of thoughts can stem from dishonesty of actions or words.

A person will begin to justify to themselves and to others that their actions or words are acceptable. Barbara, for example, would say to herself: *This grocery store makes a lot of money, so they will not notice if I steal this bag of chips.* Nancy, for her part, would say to herself: *I answered my mom truthfully when I said that I ate my lunch because I did eat the fruit.*

Many patients with an eating disorder justify their actions so much that they lose the ability to know right from wrong. As they rationalize away any intuitively guilty feelings, they can no longer tell their lies from the truth. When they convince themselves that a path without heart (a negative path) is a path with heart (a positive, loving, intuitive path), they lose their ability to tell right from wrong. A person loses the ability to listen to their intuition. They must be honest with themselves about whether they are on a positive or a negative path. Only in that way do they retain the ability to get off the negative path when they no longer like the consequences of that path.

If a patient no longer hears their intuitively truthful voice, they can still ask themselves: *Is the action I am about to take going to hurt anyone, including me?* If the answer is yes, then the patient can stop and think instead: *If I steal food, am I hurting the store owner's business? Am I hurting myself because I am perpetuating my eating disorder?*

A person who lies, steals, or cheats is not always caught. But in their conscience and soul, they must account for their actions. Everyone has moments of dishonesty. These actions may hurt someone else, but most often they hurt the person being dishonest. Acting dishonestly in words or deeds does not promote high self-esteem. The more honest people become, the better they will feel about themselves.

"No legacy is so rich as honesty."

William Shakespeare

STOP

DO NOT CONTINUE UNTIL YOU HAVE THE FOLLOWING SIGNATURES:

THERAPIST _____

DIETITIAN (RD) _____

PHYSICIAN (MD) _____

Chapter Six:
Stage Three (Participation)

Stage Three (Participation) goals

Eat 100% of meals, with no supplementation

Participate actively in groups and individual therapy

List your inner positive traits

Gain more understanding of the underlying reasons for your eating disorder

Learn about the medical complications of your eating disorder

Begin to understand anger and the concept of forgiveness

Continue to challenge your eating disorder thoughts/voice with honesty

Start using healthier coping skills

Continue to explore issues with the family

Confront your fears with courage and a belief that one can learn from life experiences

Comply with the daily points sheet

Stage Three (Participation) expectations

Nutritional Expectations

Eat 100 % of meal plan without supplements

Agree to an increase in meal plan calories if needed

No negotiating food items on menu plan with program staff or family

Reduce eating disorder rituals

Explore emotional connections with food

Follow meal and snack plans

Successfully complete meal and snack challenges in program or therapy session

Family to cook and pack all meals and snacks for program, school, or work, and supervise all meals at home

Family may be responsible for filling out the part of the daily points sheet dealing with meals and snacks when the patient is eating at home

Medical Expectations

Complete all necessary labs, urine samples, and medical appointments

Maintain medical stability (orthostatic vitals close to normal)

Begin to show steady weight gain if a patient has AN

If patient has BN, no binge-eating/purging behaviors

Read and review with MD, RD, or therapist the Medical Complications of an ED

Must not show subtle signs of exercise

Therapy Expectations

List your three goals for this stage and the ways you plan to achieve these goals

Attend and actively participate in all groups

Be honest and open about current eating disorder behaviors

Learn to express feelings appropriately

List your positive traits and make a colorful poster about them

Make a list of the reasons for your eating disorder

List positive coping skills that would be helpful in addressing each of these reasons

Talk about these reasons for your eating disorder in groups and in individual therapy

Understand your anger, and consider the concept of forgiveness

Gain more understanding of your family's positive and negative qualities

Attend and participate in family meetings

Confront your fears with courage and the belief that one can learn from life experiences

Restrictions

No exercise for patients struggling to show steady weight gain

Intensive meal monitoring for patients struggling to eat their meal plan

Patients who are not eating or drinking 100% of their meal plan may be dropped
back to a lower level

Privileges

May make some substitutions in their meal plan, such as substituting one fruit for another or one
flavor of juice, yogurt, or bread type for another

May have choice of snacks

May have meal outings with staff/RD/therapist to practice self-responsibility in ordering and eating an
appropriate meal

May have meal outings with supportive parents, family, or friends (if adult)

May be allowed to participate in minimal activity if showing steady weight gain (as approved by the
medical doctor (MD)

List your goals for Stage Three and ways that you plan to achieve these goals

1

    a

    b

    c

2

    a

    b

    c

3

    a

    b

    c

My positive traits

List qualities that you like about yourself, focusing on your inner self
Do not include anything about your body
Example: I am intelligent

1

2

3

4

5

6

7

8

9

10

Now make a colorful poster of these traits

The importance of your positive traits

Positive traits are the characteristic qualities, abilities, attitudes, and temperament that made up a patient's personality before their eating disorder took over mentally, physically, and emotionally. These traits have been present since they were very young. One of the goals of therapy is to help a patient confront their eating disorder thoughts and actions so they can take back their inherent personality.

The illnesses of anorexia nervosa and bulimia nervosa change a person's personality. These illnesses will cause a person who is inherently honest to lie about how much they have eaten or purged. A person who was friendly and outgoing will become moody, irritable, and withdrawn because the eating disorder thoughts/voice will tell them they are not worthy of having friendships. A person who was caring and giving will become so overwhelmed with their eating disorder that they become demanding and self-centered. Athletic students who have been participating in competitive sports become so weak with starvation that they are forced to stop these confidence-building activities.

Initially, when asked to list ten of their positive traits, some adults cannot write down any traits because they have been under the influence of the negative eating disorder voice for so long that they cannot remember who they were before the illness started. In a case like this, they are asked to request that a parent make a list of adjectives that would describe that person when they were five or ten years old. If no parent is available, they can ask a friend to list the positive traits that the patient no longer recognizes in themselves.

Most adolescents are able, with encouragement, to list ten positive traits. They are told, "This is who you are! Your anorexia nervosa or bulimia nervosa is an illness; it is not your identity." The adolescents are asked to make a poster of these positive traits and put it in their room. Every time the strong eating disorder thoughts/voice tells them, *you are a liar, you are stupid, you are mean, you are not worthy of friends,* the adolescent must block those negative thoughts, and repeat in their mind their positive traits: *I am honest, I am intelligent, I am caring, and I am deserving of friendships.* Eventually, by getting treatment and becoming healthier, the adolescent begins to believe in their positive traits. As a result, they are more motivated to gain to a healthy weight so that they can return to their favorite sport or reconnect with their supportive friends.

Another goal of therapy is to seek ways to build upon a person's positive traits. If a patient lists intelligence among these traits, encourage them to expand on their intellectual interests, perhaps by joining a science, literature, or computer club. If artistic talent is on a person's list, they may enjoy an art class. If they list compassion, maybe they would enjoy participating in a volunteer program. These activities build self-confidence and self-esteem, which helps the person confront any negative eating disorder thoughts.

List reasons for your eating disorder and give coping skills that would be helpful

Example *Comparing myself to other women*

Coping Skills

1 Remind myself that every person's body is unique and different

2 Remind myself to accept my body

3 Repeat my positive traits list and believe in the beauty of the inner self

4 Distract myself by listening to music or talking to a friend

5 Smile and be friendly so others will get to know my inner self

Reason one

Coping Skills

1

2

3

4

5

Reason two

Coping Skills

1

2

3

4

5

Reason three

Coping Skills

1

2

3

4

5

Reason four

Coping Skills

1

2

3

4

5

Reason five

Coping Skills

1

2

3

4

5

Symptoms and physical signs of AN and BN

Patients with eating disorders have physical signs and symptoms related to their eating disorder. Many of the complications of anorexia nervosa are secondary to starvation and can involve dysfunction in all of the major organs of the body.

Common symptoms of anorexia nervosa

Mark X in front of symptoms that you have experienced

_____Headaches

_____ Cold extremities

_____ Sleep disturbances

_____ Irritability and depression

_____ Poor concentration

_____ Abdominal pain

_____ Constipation

_____ Cold intolerance

_____ Amenorrhea

_____ Fatigue

_____ Lack of sexual interest

_____ Feeling dizzy

_____ Chest pains

Common physical signs of anorexia nervosa

Mark X in front of physical signs noted by your doctor

_____ Low body temperature

_____ Low heart rate

_____ Low blood pressure

_____ Abnormal changes in pulse or blood pressure upon standing

_____ Skeletal in appearance

_____ Arrested skeletal growth (not growing taller)

_____ Hands and feet cold to touch

_____ Hair is thin, brittle, and falls out easily

_____ Body produces soft, downy hair (lanugo)

_____ Irregular heart beat

_____ Face appears pale

_____ Dark circles under the eyes

_____ Thinking is distorted (denial of illness)

_____ Hands and feet appear red or bluish

_____ Hands appear yellow

Patients with anorexia nervosa, please answer the following.

1 Describe secret behaviors that you do to conceal your eating disorder.

2 What thoughts do you have when you deny your illness to others?

3 How do you punish yourself if you do not follow your eating disorder rules?

4 What thoughts do you have when people make you eat?

5 What thoughts do you have after you eat?

6 Describe a time when you thought that you might die.

7 How do you feel about recovering from your illness?

8 Do you think that you have distorted thoughts about your body size?

Common symptoms of bulimia nervosa

Mark X in front of symptoms that you have experienced

_____ Abdominal pain and bloating

_____ Constipation

_____ Recurrent vomiting

_____ Gastric reflux

_____ Heartburn

_____ Dental cavities

_____ Physical weakness

_____ Depression

_____ Fatigue

_____ Chest pains

Common physical signs of bulimia nervosa

Mark X in front of physical signs noted by your doctor

_____ Swollen cheeks from parotid gland swelling

_____ Gum disease from acid in vomit

_____ Erosion of dental enamel, cavities, and loss of teeth

_____ Lack of gag reflex

_____ Scars on the back of the hand (Russell's sign) from using finger to purge

_____ Swelling of hands and feet (edema)

Patients that have purged, please answer the following.

1 Describe the thoughts that you have just before you purge.

2 What are your binge-eating foods?

3 What obsessive thoughts do you have about your binge-eating/purging behaviors?

4 What are your compulsive behaviors or rituals related to your binge-eating/purging behaviors?

5 What secret behaviors do you use to conceal your vomit?

6 Have you ever vomited blood?

7 Have you experienced impulsive behaviors, such as stealing, self-harm, suicidal actions, or substance abuse?

8 Do you feel that you have severe mood swings?

Medial complications of eating disorders

Patients with eating disorders may find it helpful to understand why they have the physical signs and symptom related to their illness. The information below is designed to help patients understand the medical complications of their eating disorder. (This section's information is not comprehensive in the number of illnesses covered nor in the the details of each illness noted.)

Gastrointestinal system

Teeth

When a person vomits, it causes acidic gastric contents to come up from the stomach. This causes damage to gum tissue and softening and erosion of the tooth enamel. Patients who purge may complain of sensitivities to hot and cold food or drinks. These patients may further damage their gums and teeth by vigorously brushing their teeth after vomiting.

Parotid Glands

These glands, which are located at the angle of the jaw, can develop swelling and sometime tenderness, resulting in the patient's face having a "chipmunk" look. Some patients with BN (bulimia nervosa) develop this condition.

Esophagus

Irritation of the esophagus can result when patients stick long objects down their throat to cause vomiting. These patients may also lose their "gag" reflex. Most problems with the esophagus result from vomiting. The stomach's acidic gastric contents come back up through the esophagus, to the mouth causing possible inflammation at every level. The acidic gastric contents can cause inflammation at the junction of the stomach and esophagus (gastric reflux), then inflammation of the esophagus (esophagitis), larynx (hoarse voice), pharynx (sore throat), and gingivitis (gum swelling). Repeated vomiting can cause the lining of the esophagus to have small tears in the blood vessels, and small amounts of blood may be in the vomitus. Any blood in the vomitus should be medically evaluated. Severe and/or prolonged vomiting episodes can cause a Mallory-Weiss tear. This major tear in the lining of the esophagus results in serious bleeding, a condition that in rare instances can be fatal.

Stomach

Patients with AN (anorexia nervosa) may have delayed gastric emptying, a condition in which the food stays in the stomach longer than normal. This condition can result in the patient complaining of bloating, upper abdominal pain, feeling full, nausea, gastric flux, heartburn, and excess gas. This condition may be present before and/or after starting refeeding. Delayed gastric emptying is the result of several factors related to starvation. The malnourished body has a decrease in gastric enzymes that digest the food. In the small intestine, the villi (fingerlike projections from the surface of the intestine that increase the area for absorption of substances) have atrophied, and this causes malabsorption of important nutrients. The muscles of the stomach and the small and large intestines are impaired from lack of nutrients and use so the food is not moved efficiently through the stomach and intestines. Patients will often complain that their stomach hurts and that it has "shrunk," when what is actually the case is that the stomach is not functioning properly. After a patient has undergone refeeding and is eating normal meals, the stomach and intestinal muscles have to begin working appropriately, perhaps causing pain, like leg muscles after running a mile. In addition, the body has to produce more gastric enzymes, and the intestinal villi have to be rebuilt. This process of once again digesting healthy quantities of food can be very uncomfortable for the patient. Patients need to be encouraged to continue eating and be helped to understand that the recovery process is often uncomfortable. Delayed gastric emptying usually resolves with continued healthy eating and weight gain.

Intestine

Patients with AN may have constipation from limited food and water intake, resulting in reflex hypofunctioning (slowing) of the colon. Some patients confuse constipation with feeling full from eating, and then they refuse to finish their meal.

Patients with eating disorders may have constipation from abuse of stimulant laxatives. Patients with eating disorders initially think that laxatives will help them lose weight, or they feel "lighter" after bowel movements. Patients need to know that laxatives are an ineffective way to lose weight because laxatives work in the colon (at the end of the large intestine). Calorie absorption already occurred in the small intestine. The use or abuse of stimulant laxatives can cause serious bowel problems. Stimulant laxatives may cause tolerance with a decrease in normal bowel motility. The patient uses stimulant laxatives; the bowel motility becomes less; the patient feels more constipated and takesmore laxatives. A vicious cycle can be created. Normal bowel motility usually resumes in time once laxatives are stopped and the patient is gaining weight and eating healthy.

Gallbladder

Patients who have abruptly lost a great deal of weight have an increased possibility of getting gallstones. These patients may experience nausea and vomiting and complain of upper right abdominal pain.

Pancreas

Patients with eating disorders have occasionally had episodes of acute pancreatitis, often associated with drinking alcohol or with gallstones. Inflammation of the pancreas is a serious medical problem.

Dermatologic System

Skin

The skin can appear dry, which can be caused by many different problems, such as malnutrition, vitamin A deficiency, dehydration (from reduced fluid intake), excessive fluid elimination (from diuretic or laxative abuse), or frequent vomiting. The skin may have a yellow/orange tinge from an increased serum carotene. This may result from a defect in the liver's absorption or metabolism of carotene, or it may come from an oral intake of an excessive amount of vegetables and fruits that contain carotenoids, which is the pigment responsible for the bright red, yellow, or orange color of many fruits and vegetables. Long-term starvation can make a patient's skin look much older than normal.

Patients with BN (bulimia nervosa) may have redness or scars, called "Russell's sign," on the topside of their hands. These scars are the result of the front teeth hitting the top of the hand when a patient sticks a finger down their throat to cause vomiting. Patients with this disorder may also develop red eyes from broken blood vessels (conjunctival hemorrhages) that can be the result of repeated and/or severe vomiting.

Patients with eating disorders may have current/healing cuts and/or scars on their body from self-injurious behaviors, such as cutting or burning their skin. There is a high correlation between these self-injurious behaviors and a history of sexual abuse.

Hair/Nails

Patients who are starving have protein and nutrient deficiencies that can result in scalp hair that is thin, brittle, and of poor quality. This hair easily falls out, sometimes by the handfuls. After starting refeeding, a patient may feel dismay at seeing a lot of of hair fall out until realizing that new, healthy hair is taking its place. Because the body of a patient with AN (anorexia nervosa) has little body fat insulation, it often produces soft, pale colored body and facial hair that can help insulate the body and keep it warm. This hair is called lanugo. The nails of a patient with AN are often thin, brittle, and dry.

Skeletal system

Bones

The patient with AN who has been restricting food intake and losing weight may begin to have bone loss (osteopenia) before they experience loss of their menstrual period (amenorrhea). After months, or years, of amenorrhea, many patients develop (osteoporosis), which is severe thinning of the bones. The resultant decrease in bone mass, often in the hips and lumbar spine (lower back), is related to a depletion of calcium and bone protein. Patients with osteopenia or osteoporosis may have bone pain when they exercise, and they have a much higher incidence of breaking a bone. Restoring periods begins the process of rebuilding bones, but it is gaining to a healthy weight that results in the best bone growth, since body weight is an important factor in bone density. Most skeletal bone growth is in childhood and adolescence and usually ends by the mid 20s. The bones of a patient with AN may never return to normal. A person in their 30s with long-term AN may have the bone mineral density of a much older person. Males with AN are also at risk for loss of bone density.

Patients with AN may receive a DXA scan (dual energy x-ray absorptiometry) to measure bone mineral density. A DXA scan can help patients with AN become aware of how much bone loss is occurring as a result of their AN.

Cardiovascular system

Bradycardia (low heart rate)

The normal heart rate is 60-99 beats per minute. In bradycardia, the heart rate is less than 60 beats per minute. Patients with the diagnosis of AN who have a very low weight usually have a low heart rate, often below 50 beats per minute. At this low heart rate, some patients may complain of chest pain and shortness of breath. As the heart rate gets very low (<40) the possibility of severe cardiac problems rises. Anorexia nervosa has the highest mortality of any psychiatric disorder (Arcelus et al., 2011). Deaths are often due to cardiovascular complications.

Hypotension (low blood pressure)

Hypotension is defined as a systolic BP less than 90 mmHg and/or a diastolic BP less than 60mmHg. When starved over time, the body begins to conserve energy by slowing the heart rate, lowering the body temperature, and lowering the blood pressure. With continued starvation, the body uses up the fat stores and begins to use muscle as a source of energy. The loss of cardiac muscle mass causes a decrease in cardiac output, which results in a lower blood pressure. Patients with this condition complain of a reduced exercise capacity and fatigue. When such a person exercises or even stands up, the damaged heart cannot beat harder so it beats faster, causing the pulse rate to go up and the blood pressure to drop even lower. Many patients with hypotension may feel light-headed or dizzy; they may even faint (pass out) when they stand up.

Orthostatic changes

A patient's pulse and blood pressure are measured while lying and then while standing. The difference between the lying and standing values is called orthostatic changes. This difference is an indication of how well the heart is performing. A pulse change that is greater than 35 from lying to standing (e.g., a pulse change from 50 lying to 90 standing) is considered abnormal. Likewise, a blood pressure drop in systolic blood pressure of > 20 mmHg in adults and >10mmHg in adolescents from lying to standing (e.g., 100/64 mmHg lying to 75/49 mmHg standing) is considered abnormal. These orthostatic changes are often slow to improve with weight restoration.

Patients with AN who have a low heart rate may claim that their heart rate is so low because they are athletic and exercise excessively; but when measured, their heart rate increases dramatically when they stand. A healthy, athletic person's heart rate may be low normal, but it increases only minimally when they stand up.

Many patients with eating disorders have a compulsive need to exercise, often to excess. They may go to the gym and work out for hours, or run for hours, often without eating any food before or after these activities. Patients with eating disorders will burn extra calories by constantly standing, or keep their legs in motion if sitting. Excessive exercise is dangerous for patients with AN because it uses calories that the starved body needs to keep the heart adequately nourished. Stressing a malnourished body with strenuous exercise can cause serious medical complications.

Hypothermia (low temperature)
A normal body temperature is 98.6 F. A patient with severe AN can have a low body temperature (less than 97F) because the body is trying to conserve energy. A patient's hands and feet may appear bluish (acrocyanosis) and are cold to the touch. These symptoms are related to low body temperature and to the the body's restricting blood flow to the extremities.

Mitral valve prolapse
This condition may occur more often in patients with AN than in the general population. Mitral valve prolapse is thought to occur when the heart wall decreases with starvation, with no change in the size of the mitral valve. This can cause the mitral valve not to close properly. Patients with this condition may complain of fatigue, light-headedness, chest pains, or palpitations (perceived feelings of an irregular, or strong, or rapid heart rate).

Conditions detected by an EKG (electrocardiogram)
Cardiac arrhythmias (abnormal heart rhythms) on an EKG of a patient with an ED can be related to several causes, including electrolyte abnormalities, effects of certain medications, or changes in the heart muscle from starvation. Cardiac arrhythmias can be fatal.

Cardiomyopathy
Cardiomyopathy is a disease in which the heart muscle becomes enlarged, thick, and rigid. This condition can stem from the use by patients of ipecac to induce vomiting. Cardiomyopathy is a serious cardiac condition.

Reproductive system

Amenorrhea

Amenorrhea is defined as no menstrual periods for at least three consecutive cycles. It can be caused by low body weight (from restrictive eating), emotional stress, or excessive exercise. Some patients with AN stop menstruating before they lose a significant amount of weight (Igra, 2000). Patients often begin restricting by eliminating fats, which can lead to decreased estrogen production, resulting in the loss of menses. Some girls like that they no longer have menses, and that their hips and breasts are not developing. They think that these physical features are often associated with being fat. Low estrogen production not only affects menses, but also affects healthy bone development, which can result in shorter stature, pubertal delay, and bone fractures. Estrogen, along with Vitamin D, helps the body absorb the calcium that builds strong, healthy bones. Return of menses generally occurs within six months of a patient gaining to 90% of healthy body weight, if the patient's body is making adequate estradiol (Igra, 2000). Adolescents often become focused on what they weighed when their menses returned and do not want to gain any further weight, even if they are not at their healthy body weight. The body develops healthier bone when the person is at their healthy body weight. Adolescents may need to be reminded that each year, as they grow and mature, they will need to continue to gain to a healthy body weight for their menses to continue, and to have healthy bone development.

Some athletes will say they have no menses because they are exercising so much to be competitive in their sport. In reality, many of these athletes are not menstruating because they are not eating enough food each day. Athletes sometimes admit that they were restricting because they thought they would be a faster runner or swimmer if they lost a few pounds. When athletes begin restricting, it can be very dangerous because they often have low body fat stores. If the athlete does not eat enough food to supply adequate glucose for the body, and they have few fat stores, the body begins to use muscle as a source of energy. The heart muscle can be one of the first muscles to be used for energy. Skeletal muscles are also used as energy; and they begin to look wasted and have no tone. Exercise will not build muscle when the body is starved and does not have enough calories, protein and other nutrients to build muscle.

Patients with BN often have menstrual irregularities and they can have amenorrhea (no menses). Most patients with BN do not have delayed sexual development or stunted stature.

Pregnancy

Women with a diagnoses of an eating disorder who become pregnant may be more at risk for some perinatal complications (Pasternak et al., 2012). Some women may be reluctant to tell their physician about their past or current eating disorder. It is important that pregnant women with an eating disorder be closely monitored by a multi-disciplinary treatment team during their pregnancy to get the best possible outcome for both the mother and the child (Mehler and Andersen, 2017). Patients with past or active eating disorders who become pregnant have an increased risk of a premature birth infant, a low birth weight infant, or an infant with a smaller head circumference (Koubaa et al., 2008). A pregnant patient with a current history of eating disorder symptoms and a history of past depression has an increased risk for depression and anxiety both before the baby is born and for postpartum depression (Micali et al., 2011).

Males

Starvation in males results in a decrease in serum testosterone, which can lead to delayed sexual development, decreased sex drive, muscle wasting, and possible growth retardation. Males with anorexia nervosa can have osteopenia or osteoporosis (decreased bone mineral density) related to their restricted food intake (Mehler and Anderson, 2017).

Neurologic System

Conditions detected by MRI studies

Patients who are severely restricting their food may not be providing the appropriate amount of glucose to the brain. The brain needs glucose (sugar) to function. Patients with AN are not only starving their body, they are starving their brain. Also, if a person has a very slow heart rate, they may deprive the brain of oxygen. MRI studies of patients with anorexia nervosa show increased cerebrospinal fluid and decreased brain volume with a reduction of both gray and white matter (Titoya et al., 2013). The longer a person has low weight caused by AN, the more likely the brain changes will be permanent.

Cognitive deficits

A patient with severe malnutrition may present with a blunted affect, slowed responses to questions, poor concentration, difficulty switching tasks, and impaired problem solving. Starvation can make a patient anxious, irritable, moody, and depressed. Patients with AN have sleep difficulties and frequently wake up at night because they are hungry. Patients with AN have a distorted body image; they see themselves as fat, even though they are very thin. A patient who gains to a healthy weight may still have a persistence of the body image distortion. A patient with AN may also have distorted thinking concerning their illness, believing that they are "fine" when they are actually very ill medically.

Endocrine system

The thyroid gland is a butterfly-shaped endocrine gland in the neck. It produces and stores hormones that affect almost every organ in the body. The thyroid's main role is to regulate the body's metabolism (breakdown of food to energy). During starvation, the body tries to compensate for the lack of adequate food by lowering the body's energy needs. The body decreases the heart rate, body temperature, thyroid hormone production (including TSH), and blood flow to the gut and the extremities. Patients may complain of dry skin, constipation, fatigue, and cold intolerance. They feel the need to wear sweaters and coats much of the time. The thyroid hormone production, (including TSH) usually returns to normal with eating appropriately and gaining to a healthy weight.

The starvation state in AN can cause the body to be in a constant state of stress, causing an elevated blood cortisol level (hypercortisolemia) in the body. Normally, cortisol is produced in acute situations or in a major life crisis, in what is known as the "flight-or-fight" reaction. When the stress passes, the cortisol level drops. This hypercortisolemia in patients with AN has been associated with bone loss and depression. (Lawson et al. 2009)

Hematologic system

Most patients with an AN will have normal blood counts. Some patients with AN have a decrease in red blood cells (anemia) from poor intake of iron, folate, or vitamin B12. These patients can complain of pale skin, fatigue, shortness of breath, and dizziness. Some patients with AN have low white blood cell counts (leukopenia) which can interfere with the body's ability to fight infection. A patient that is bruising easily may have a low platelet count (thrombocytopenia). Blood cells are made in the bone marrow. A patient's blood cell counts often return to normal soon after the patient is getting adequate, healthy nutrition, even before showing much weight gain.

Renal (Kidney) system

Patients with eating disorders can have abnormal renal labs, especially during times of severe dehydration or excessive water intake. For example, they can have changes in their urine. If a patient has been water loading in order to show weight gain, the urine specific gravity may be low (<1.010). A urine ph that is high (8-9) may suggest that the patient has been purging.

Electrolyte disturbances

Electrolytes are usually normal in patients with AN, unless they are water loading, in the process of refeeding, or covertly purging while denying this behavior. Patients with AN use normal labs as a way to reinforce their statements that they are "fine," when they often are very medically ill. Patients with BN frequently have electrolyte abnormalities that are related to their self-induced vomiting, diuretic misuse, and laxative abuse.

Refeeding syndrome

Patients with AN who are at a very low weight are most likely to develop this syndrome. The refeeding syndrome is a serious condition, characterized by electrolyte and fluid shifts associated with metabolic abnormalities in malnourished patients undergoing refeeding. These patients have been restricting their food intake for months or years, and their bodies have become used to having lower glucose levels. When they are refed, they take in a much higher calorie count than before. Their meals, when digested, result in more glucose in the blood stream. Insulin levels rise rapidly to pull the glucose and other electrolytes, like phosphorus, into the cells that use phosphate to make the energy necessary for the cells to rebuild. The result of the dangerous drop in phosphate in the blood is that there is now an insufficient level for the heart muscle to use to make energy in the heart cells and for the muscle to cause contraction. The result can be cardiovascular collapse and death. At the same time, potassium and magnesium are also pulled into the cells, and their deficiencies in the blood can cause additional problems. For all these reasons, patients who are being refed will get frequent blood tests to monitor their electrolytes, so that replacement electrolytes can be given if needed.

There is yet another cardiac complication of refeeding. A patient with severe AN does not eat enough calories to sustain their body, so the body begins destroying the cardiac muscle as a source of fuel. The cardiac muscle becomes thinner and less able to provide normal cardiac output. When a patient is refed, they eat and drink more, which increases the amount of fluid in the blood stream. The heart muscle is unable to handle this increased load of fluid, a situation that can lead to congestive heart failure and death. Your cardiac vital signs will be closely monitored during refeeding.

Patients who are being refed can develop edema (swelling) in their lower legs or abdomen, which can be quite distressing. This edema resolves with continued weight gain. Patients with BN often develop edema from purging or when they stop taking laxatives after long-term abuse of laxatives.

Medical complications quiz

1 Osteoporosis occurs in the _____.

2 The _____ shows arrhythmias of the heart.

3 Severe vomiting can cause a rare condition called a _____ tear.

4 _____ is the lack of menstrual periods.

5 In anorexia, _____ can fall out by the handfuls.

6 Abnormal functioning of the _____ gland causes slow heart rate, constipation, dry skin, and cold intolerance.

7 _____ is necessary for strong bones.

8 _____ can cause cardiomyopathy.

9 Low body weight, fear of gaining weight, and a distorted body image describes the illness of _____.

10 Patients with _____ have pale skin, fatigue, shortness of breath, and dizziness.

11 Swelling and puffiness around the ankles and feet is called_____.

12 _____ is stored in the gallbladder and emulsifies fats in the small intestine.

13 The _____ glands can become swollen and painful in patients who purge.

14 Patients with anorexia have low levels of the female hormone _____.

15 Bone mineral density can be measured by a _____.

16 Scars on the back of the hand related to self-induced vomiting _____.

17 The _____ studies show that the volume of gray and white matter is reduced in the brains of patients with AN.

18 Patients with AN produce soft, pale colored hair called _____.

19 Starvation causes a low heart rate, called _____, in patients with AN.

20 Patients with BN frequently have damage to their _____ enamel.

Medical complications quiz (answers)

1   Osteoporosis occurs in the **bones**

2   The **EKG** shows arrhythmias of the heart.

3   Severe vomiting can cause a rare condition called a **Mallory-Weiss** tear.

4   **Amenorrhea** is the lack of menstrual periods.

5   In anorexia, **hair** can fall out by the handfuls.

6   Abnormal functioning of the **thyroid** gland causes slow heart rate, constipation, dry skin, and cold intolerance.

7   **Calcium** is necessary for strong bones.

8   **Ipecac** can cause cardiomyopathy.

9   Low body weight, fear of gaining weight, and a distorted body image describes the illness of **anorexia nervosa (AN)**.

10 Patients with **anemia** have pale skin, fatigue, shortness of breath, and dizziness.

11 Swelling and puffiness around the ankles and feet is called **edema**.

12 **Bile** is stored in the gallbladder and emulsifies fats in the small intestine.

13 The **parotid** glands can become swollen and painful in patients who purge.

14 Patients with anorexia have low levels of the female hormone **estrogen**.

15 Bone mineral density can be measured by a **DXA Scan**.

16 Scars on the back of the hand related to self-induced vomiting **Russell's sign**.

17 The **MRI** studies show that the volume of gray and white matter is reduced in the brains of patients with AN.

18 Patients with AN produce soft, pale colored hair called **lanugo.**

19 Starvation causes a low heart rate, called **bradycardia**, in patients with AN.

20 Patients with BN frequently have damage to their **tooth** enamel.

Indications for immeadiate referral for a medical examination

From history

Dizziness upon standing

Fainting

Chest pain

Starvation with no food intake in 72 hours

No fluid intake in 48 hours

Precipitous weight loss

Excessive use of diuretics or laxatives

Excessive vomiting (many times a day)

Blood in the vomitus

Seizures

Severe cramping in hands and feet

From Observation

Cognitive slowing or impaired concentration

Extreme thinness/emaciation

Low temperature < 97F

Heart rate <50 beats per minute

Heart rate increase of >20 from lying to standing

Systolic blood pressure drop of > 10mmHG in adolescents and >20mmHG in adults from
lying to standing

As part of the medical examination, the patient will have EKG and blood tests done.

Anger questionnaire

How often do you agree with each statement

1 = Never   2 = Sometimes   3 = Frequently   4 = Always

1   I yell at my parents when I am angry ____

2   I have episodes of binge eating when I am angry ____

3   I purge when I am angry ____

4   My husband yells at me when he is angry ____

5   My parents yell at each other ____

6   I do not feel comfortable expressing my anger ____

7   When I am angry, I feel like hurting myself ____

8   I get angry with myself when I eat ____

9   I get angry when people tell me to eat ____

10 I get angry about past abuse ____

11 I get angry when my boss yells at me ____

12 I feel like hurting the person that makes me angry ____

13 My father is easily angered ____

14 I feel angry that my life is so difficult ____

15 I get angry with myself when I feel inadequate ____

16 I throw or break things when I am angry ____

17 I have lost friends because of my anger ____

18 I hold in my anger and then explode over minor issues ____

19 I feel angry when I am not in control ____

20 I get angry when I am teased at school ____

21 I feel angry when I am ignored ____

22 I feel angry that my family does not understand my eating disorder ____

23 I get angry with myself when I lie ____

24 I get angry when I hurt my body ___

25 I get angry when my friends try to "fix me" ____

26 When I am angry I feel powerful ____

27 I get angry when I gain weight ____

28 I get angry when people expect me to be perfect ____

29 I wish I had better coping skills to deal with my anger ____

30 I get angry when my friends do not understand my eating disorder ____

31 When I am lonely I get angry ____

32 I get angry when my friends embarrass me ____

33 I wish that I could be more assertive without resorting to anger ____

34 I feel angry when people comment about how I look ____

35 I feel angry that my spouse blames me for everything ____

36 I withdraw from people when they are angry with me ____

37 I say mean things when I get angry ____

38 I get angry when I am afraid ____

39 I get angry that the doctor will not tell me my weight ____

Draw a picture or write an essay about your anger

Describe situations that have made you very angry
How did you respond?

Example:
situation: I was raped and threatened by a neighborhood man
response: I was scared. I did not tell. I felt empty, like my soul had been stolen

1 situation:

  response:

2 situation:

  response:

3 situation

  response

4 situation

  response

Anger and forgiveness

Anger is a normal response to hurting one's body, soul, or pride. If anger is not addressed or if the hurt is too great, a patient may begin to feel hatred towards the source of the anger. These strong negative feelings are a great burden to those who carry them. Such feelings can prevent one from following a positive path. Each patient must deal with negative feelings that erode their body and soul. Negative actions in one's past can become negative forces in their present. Although past events cannot be changed, they can be viewed in a new light. Because anger is a secondary emotion, one can understand their anger by looking at the hurt.

Jane's example

Jane is an 38-year-old woman with bulimia nervosa, divorced parents, and a history of abandonment and sexual abuse. This abuse has caused Jane to be sensitive to any real or perceived rejection, abandonment, or criticism. One day, her therapist was late for a session. Jane became enraged and began verbally criticizing the therapist for his past comments and actions. Initially, the therapist was puzzled by Jane's response, but then he realized that Jane perceived his tardiness as another personal rejection in her life. The therapist apologized for his lateness, helped Jane to understand why she had become so angry and how she could retrain her thinking so as to be less sensitive to rejection and criticism.

In order to forgive, one must let go of any judgments that they may have about another person. Forgiveness is blocked by anger, and anger is rooted in judgment. Judgment is a belief that one's anger is justified as a punishment towards another person. Trying to understand the other person may help one let go of judgment—and therefore anger—against that person.

Many patients with eating disorders have suffered terrible traumas or long-term emotional, physical, and sexual abuse. Overwhelming pain and anger can transform into anger at oneself, which can lead to drug and alcohol abuse, suicidal actions, eating disorders, and cutting. Such actions and anger keep a patient anchored in their past. Therapy is a necessary step in lifting that anchor.

Abuse or trauma can be so terrible that a person may not believe themselves able to forgive another person. However, forgiveness is not only something that is done for others. Forgiveness is something that one does for themselves. A person makes the choice to let go of anger and resentment once they realize that carrying negative feelings ultimately hurts themselves more than anyone else. Not only does anger keep one anchored to the past, anger can make a person mentally and physically ill. People with anger are more likely to suffer depression, heart attack, stroke, and a poor immune system. Forgiveness of others and of self allows a person to heal mind and body and to move forward in life.

"Anger is an acid that can do more harm to the vessel
in which it is stored that to anything on which it is poured."

Mark Twain

Your parents

Father's positive qualities   Father's negative qualities

Mother's positive qualities   Mother's negative qualities

Family's positive and negative comments

What has your father said that affected you positively?

What has your father said that affected you negatively?

What has your mother said that affected you positively?

What has your mother said that affected you negatively?

What has your spouse, significant other, or sib said that affected you positively?

What has your spouse, significant other, or sib said that affected you negatively?

What issues do you want to discuss with your family in the next family session?

1

2

3

4

Write a letter to your family commenting on how you think your eating disorder has affected them

Fear, courage, and lessons learned

What lessons have you learned from your life experiences?
Example: Spreading gossip hurts others, and me

1

2

3

4

5

List times when you were afraid

1

2

3

List times when you showed courage

1

2

3

Confronting fear with courage and a belief that one can learn from life's experiences

Being cautious in dangerous situations is a rational response to fear. For instance, it is reasonable to lock doors at night to discourage intruders. It is reasonable to drive carefully on rainy days to prevent accidents. However, fear is not always rational. A person with an eating disorder may be afraid that they will not be popular if they are not thin. They fear that they are not perfect. Fear of losing control of their life causes them to control their eating. These are examples of irrational fears related to an eating disorder belief.

Patients with eating disorders are sensitive to uncertainties in their life. They try to eliminate fear by eliminating uncertainty. They try to change or control situations that are out of their hands, such as the relationship between their parents. Fear of the unknown leaves patients with a helpless, haunting feeling that causes sleepless nights and increased stress.

Life involves learning to live with uncertainty. A patient can learn to confront this inevitable uncertainty with courage and the belief that they can learn from their experiences. Courage is not the absence of fear, but rather the mastering of one's fears.

Example 1: Allison

Allison is afraid to tell her family that she is purging because she is fearful of their reaction. She avoids the problem by hiding all evidence of her eating disorder. But if Allison admits to purging, she has the opportunity to grow into an honest person. If she fears everything that happens from the consequences of telling the truth, then she moves further away from the goal. If Allison confronts the uncertainty with courage, she will experience freedom from her fear. Learning to confront the fear of her parents' anger will allow her to have the courage to confront difficult situations in the future.

People must come to believe that they can learn from life's experiences, both good and bad.

Example 2: Melissa

Melissa has suffered from anorexia nervosa since college, and she is fearful that she will never recover. In the process of treatment, Melissa starts to talk about her fears and begins to confront her strong eating disorder voice. She begins to believe that she can recover. Melissa begins to understand the dynamics of her illness and its underlying causes. She realizes that she can learn and grow from the terrible experience of having an illness.

Even when a patient feels stuck in their eating disorder, they can ask: *What can I learn from this situation?* Some patients feel sorry for themselves or seek to place blame on others. Other patients look within themselves and see the opportunity for inner enrichment. An eating disorder presents a patient with lessons that will enrich their life.

Example 3: The pessimistic child and the optimistic child

The pessimistic child is shown a room full of toys. The child walks into the room and critically examines each item. He is afraid that he will not find what he wants. Nothing makes him happy. Finally, in disgust, he asks: "Where is the toy train?"

The optimistic child is shown a room filled with horse manure. With a twinkle in his eye, he runs towards the pile of manure, frantically starts to dig, and says: "I know there is a pony in here somewhere!"

When patients overwhelmed by their eating disorder or are disappointed by what life has put in front of them, they must remind themselves: *Just keep looking for the pony!*

An unhealthy person believes that happiness is the absence of any misery or pain. A healthy person recognizes that some painful experiences are part of life. Happiness comes from overcoming these experiences.

"Nothing in life is to be feared, it is only to be understood."

Marie Curie

STOP

DO NOT CONTINUE UNTIL YOU HAVE THE FOLLOWING SIGNATURES:

THERAPIST _____

DIETITIAN (RD) _____

PHYSICIAN (MD) _____

Chapter Seven:
Stage Four (Action)

Stage Four (Action) goals

Eat 100% of meals and snacks with few eating disorder rituals

Actively participate in groups and/or sessions and take a leadership role

Be willing to make positive changes in thinking and behavior

Understand the cultural influences on body image

Continue to build self-acceptance

Understand triggers for restricting food intake or having binge-eating/purging behaviors

Have improved relationships with family

Work on recovery goals

Stage Four (Action) expectations

Nutritional Expectations

Eat 100% of meals and snacks

If patient skips a snack, or part of a meal, they will be honest with themselves and make up the missed calories at the next meal or at the evening snack.

Have few food rituals and work on eliminating all food rituals

Maintain normal conversation while eating

Confront and/or support peers during meals or snacks at program

Bring a weekly taboo food to program or therapy and eat it without supplementation

Take on increasing responsibilities about meal preparation at home and in the program

Successfully go to restaurants, order, and eat an appropriate meal, with supervision

Family to continue to do points sheet when patient is at home or when eating out with patient

Patient on honor to fill out points sheet for unsupervised meals when away from home or program

Medical Expectations

Complete all blood and urine sample and medical appointments as needed

Medically stable with stable vitals

If patient has BN, no binge-eating/purging behaviors

If patient has AN, they will have reached 95% of expected weight gain

May become more active in life (as approved by MD)

Therapy Expectations

List three goals for this stage and the ways you plan to achieve these goals

Be actively involved in therapy and recovery process

Take leadership in groups and confront peers on eating disorder behaviors

Learn about the cultural influences on body image

Continue to build self-acceptance

Take steps toward a positive body image

Write an essay on how you will practice self-acceptance

Take some responsibility for the path your life takes

Disengage from unhealthy people in your life

Identify triggers that would lead you to restrict or have binge-eating/purging behaviors, and develop coping skills for each trigger.

Continue to have improved relationships with family and friends

List recovery goals

Privilages

May begin planning snacks or meals on own

Not subject to observation while in program, at the discretion of the treatment team

May start having unsupervised meals with supportive friends

May have passes out of program for family trips or school activities

List your goals for Stage Four and ways that you plan to achieve these goals

1

    a

    b

    c

2

    a

    b

    c

3

    a

    b

    c

Cultural influences on body image and learning self-acceptance

Cultural influences from television, movies, and magazines have a major impact on how people view their bodies. In particular, television advertisements operate on a theory of deficiency, in which the viewer is told that they are not good enough unless they use a certain beauty product. Print advertisements often feature airbrushed, computer-altered models to sell unattainable standards of beauty. Looking at thin models in fashion magazines can cause many adolescents and adults to feel depressed, guilty, or ashamed. When a customer uses the beauty product but does not look exactly like the model in the advertisement, the customer feels like a failure. Their self-esteem and body image acceptance have been lowered. Instead of thinking: *I do not feel good about myself*, the customer may think: *I am not thin enough. Being skinny is important to being beautiful.* Therefore, a customer's emotional issues can be focused into one measurable entity: weight.

Junior High School is a time when adolescents are trying to be accepted, a time when they think that how one looks can define their status. For instance, they believe that unless you are thin, the popular girls will not talk to you. Girls may restrict their food intake to the point where they become ill with AN. Some popular girls have been known to eat lunch together and then go as a group to the bathroom to purge.

During puberty, adolescents experience many changes in their bodies, including a gain in body fat. Those who attempt unsuccessfully to stay "thin" during puberty may experience feelings of failure, negative self-image, and low self-esteem. Teasing or pressure from peers or adults at this difficult stage of physical growth can be emotionally damaging.

Patients with eating disorders usually have low self-esteem and a distorted body image. They are unable to accept who they are or how their body looks. To recover from an eating disorder, patients must develop self-acceptance of who they are mentally, emotionally, and physically. One of the first steps to improving self-esteem and developing a positive body image is to acknowledge that body shape and size is mostly determined by genetics. Despite what advertisements and commercials show, the ability to control one's body shape is limited.

Self-acceptance builds self-esteem and leads to a positive body image. Self-acceptance starts with accepting your own body and learning to respect all people regardless of their size. People tend to focus on how they look on the outside rather than giving credit to who they are on the inside. A patient will learn to appreciate their many positive traits, and not focus on how they look. They will begin to enjoy their own sense of individuality and respect all those qualities that make them special. They will learn to make the most of what they have been given. It is important for a person to discover their inner beauty and uniqueness.

"The worst loneliness is to not be comfortable with yourself."

Mark Twain

List of people that I admire and why

1

2

3

4

5

Body image

Body image develops from birth by the way our bodies are treated by others. We are affected by the attitudes that family members have toward their own bodies. We can also be influenced by adults and friends who make comments about our bodies.

1   What are the negative messages you give to yourself about your body?

2   How did you feel about your body when you were younger?

3   What are some ways you have tried to change your body because you don't like it?

4   Do you have a family member who is critical of their body? What do they say about it?

5   Has anyone in your family made negative comments about your body? What did they say?

6   When you compare your body to other people's bodies, how do you feel and what thoughts do you have?

7   What do you like about your body? Why?

Write a letter to your body

Have your body write a letter to you

List reasons why your opinion of yourself should not be determined by other people

1

2

3

4

5

List reasons why your opinion of yourself should not be determined by other people

Steps toward a positive body image

1 I will accept my body.
2 I understand that there are things about my body that I cannot change.
3 I will not focus on how I look physically.
4 I will eat a healthy menu plan.
5 I will not deprive myself of foods that I love, even if they contain fat.
6 I will wear the correct size of clothing.
7 I will get rid of the clothes I had when I was ill, including the jeans.
8 I will exercise in a healthy manner.
9 I will not allow a scale to measure my self-esteem.
10 I will not make negative body comments (e.g., "My thighs are fat.").
11 I will not spend excessive time in front of the mirror.
12 I will stop talking about weight and calories.
13 I will accept compliments without thinking about my weight.
14 I will respect all people regardless of their size.
15 I will focus on the inner rather than outer attributes of people that I meet.
16 I will find positive role models.
17 I will be optimistic about my future.
18 I will be open to new information and experiences.
19 I will cherish the positive aspects of my life.
20 I will smile!

List activities that you are proud of

1

2

3

4

5

6

7

8

9

10

Write an essay about how you will practice self-acceptance

Responsibility for the path your life takes

You have some responsibility for the path your life takes. Some people just drift along in life, even though they do not like what has happened in their lives. Other people are very unhappy, and they seek to blame someone else for their misfortune. They may blame their parents, their friends, their school, their work, or negative events that have happened to them.

As long as you blame someone else, it will be difficult for you to be on a positive path. As long as you see the problem with your life as being someone else's, you will not see any need to change yourself. If you want to change your life, you must start by changing yourself. The only person that you can change is yourself. You can begin to take responsibility by starting to make things different.

You are responsible for growing, and you grow by learning new things. To live is to grow, and to change physically, intellectually, socially, and emotionally. Of course, you will make mistakes. No one can learn without making mistakes. The good news is that if you take responsibility for learning from these mistakes, you will grow.

Example: Megan wants to learn the new physical skill of riding a bike. It could just as well be an intellectual skill (like learning CBT), a social skill (like learning to be assertive), or an emotional skill (like practicing self-acceptance). In this case Megan's goal is to learn a new physical skill. As her first step, Megan climbs on the bike and points it down the road. Megan is so scared that her teeth start to chatter, but she knows that she cannot learn to ride a bike if she does not try. All seems to go well for about a hundred feet, but then she hits a bump in the road, and the bike tips over. Now she is sitting in the middle of the street. What will she do next? She can give up, pick up the bike, and walk the bike back home, blaming the bump in the road for causing this accident. Or she can admit she made a mistake, realize that she needs to hold onto the handles tighter, climb back onto the bike, and continue down the road. Gradually, by mistake after mistake, trial after trial, she will learn how to ride the bike. The quicker she learns not to make the same mistake twice, the faster she becomes a good bike rider.

It is not easy to grow. It is not easy to make mistakes and learn from them. A person may instead become resentful. When people are afraid to change, their fear can turn to anger, causing them to lash out at others. Other people have little confidence in their ability to try something new. They may lack self-confidence because they were criticized as a child, because they have experienced major tragedies in their life, or for many other reasons. A person cannot grow simply by wishing things were different. A person does not grow by staying stuck in old, unhealthy habits and behaviors. A person grows and learns by facing the problems they fear with courage, while at the same time believing that they can learn from experience.

Each person is responsible for seeing life as meaningful. With help individuals can begin to see how to deal with their problems. They come to recognize that many of the difficult situations they find themselves in are opportunities to grow, and that seeing them as such is the key to finding the meaning that is always present within them.

Invictus
William Ernest Henley

Out of the night that covers me,
Black as the Pit from pole to pole,
I thank whatever gods may be
For my unconquerable soul.

In the fell clutch of circumstance
I have not winced nor cried aloud.
Under the bludgeonings of chance
My head is bloody, but unbowed.

Beyond this place of wrath and tears
Looms but the horror of the shade,
And yet the menace of the years
Finds, and shall find me, unafraid.

It matters not how strait the gate,
How charged with punishments the scroll,
I am the master of my fate;
I am the captain of my soul.

List your recovery goals
Example: Maintain my healthy weight

1

2

3

4

5

6

7

8

9

10

Dealing with the triggers to restrict or have binge-eating/purging episodes

In this activity, you will be indentifying five triggers that lead you to restrict or have binge-eating/purging episodes. You will then identify five coping skills that help you deal with each trigger.

Example *Feeling anxious*

Coping Skills

1 Write in my journal about why I am feeling so anxious.

2 Use my cognitive behavioral therapy skills.

3 Breathe deeply and relax.

4 Talk to my therapist or family abut how I am feeling.

5 Take a hot bath to calm myself and reduce tension in my body.

First trigger

Coping Skills for your first trigger

1

2

3

4

5

Second trigger

Coping Skills for your second trigger

1

2

3

4

5

Third trigger

Coping Skills for your third trigger

1

2

3

4

5

Fourth trigger

Coping Skills for your fourth trigger

1

2

3

4

5

Fifth trigger

Coping Skills for your fifth trigger

1

2

3

4

5

List ways your family can show they care about you
Example: I want them to listen when I talk to them

1

2

3

4

5

6

7

8

9

10

Lessons from family and friends

Family and friends present a person with opportunities to learn life lessons. An adolescent who is judgmental like their parent can learn that they do not have to be judgmental of others. They can choose to change in themselves the thoughts or actions that they dislike in their parent. The adolescent can learn to express their feelings and thoughts in a more positive way and be more tolerant of the behavior of others. In this process, the adolescent feels more accepting of themselves and they can be more accepting of a parent or a friend.

What lessons do you think you can learn from your father?

1

2

3

What lessons do you think you can learn from your mother?

1

2

3

What lessons do you think you can learn from other family members, such as your spouse or siblings?

1

2

3

4

5

Write about a friend from whom you have learned the most

List the positive traits of the adult from whom you have learned the most

1

2

3

4

5

6

"There is a destiny that makes us brothers
None goes his way alone.
All that we send into the lives of others
Comes back into our own."

Edwin Markham

STOP

DO NOT CONTINUE UNTIL YOU HAVE THE FOLLOWING SIGNATURES:

THERAPIST _____

DIETITIAN (RD) _____

PHYSICIAN (MD) _____

Chapter Eight:
Stage Five (Discharge)

Stage Five (Discharge) goals

Eat 100% of meals with no rituals

Become committed to recovery

List how family and friends can be helpful in recovery

Make plans for future positive activities

Learn the importance of perseverance while in treatment that may last for years

Work on relapse prevention

Learn the value of Intuition

Stage Five (Discharge) expectations

Nutritional Expectations

Eat 100% of meal plan with no food rituals

Eat many of your prior taboo foods

Plan, prepare and consume at least one meal or snack unsupervised each day

Be able to eat out at a restaurant and have flexibility in food ordered, so as to achieve variety

Medical Expectations

Medically stable with normal vitals

Reach healthy goal weight

Continue to have regular weights and vitals as recommended by MD after discharge

May have increased activities, with set guidelines and goals as recommended by MD

Therapy Expectations

List three goals for this stage and ways that you plan to achieve these goals

Develop a treatment plan for long term outpatient therapy

Be a good role model for other patients in the eating disorder program

Answer Factors of Recovery questionnaire

List how family and friends can help you continue your recovery

Learn the importance of Intuition

Write a letter saying goodbye to your eating disorder

Perseverance essay

Study What is Recovery chart and make changes to follow those guidelines, including no mirrors, no scales, no old jeans worn in the home

Show good insight into the causes of your eating disorder

Have helpful coping skills for eating disorder thoughts or behaviors that may arise

Share recovery plans with family or friends

List and make plans for future positive activities

Study Signs of Relapse

Discharge

Privilages

Decrease in the number of days per week attending program, or continue in less intensive individual therapy

Begin to explore the return to (or further return to) school, work, or volunteer opportunities

List your goals for Stage Five and ways that you plan to achieve these goals

1

    a

    b

    c

2

    a

    b

    c

3

    a

    b

    c

Factors of recovery

Write yes or no for each of the following

1   My family will be supportive of my recovery when I get home _____

2   My therapist is understanding _____

3   I have gained self-esteem _____

4   I participate in a sport or activity that will keep me motivated _____

5   I have developed coping skills _____

6   I look forward to returning to school/work _____

7   I want to meet with a registered dietitian on a regular basis _____

8   I am willing to ask for support _____

9   I am committed to attending therapy _____

10 I want my friends and family to understand what I am going through _____

11 I have disengaged from friends that are not a positive influence _____

12 I will keep a healthy weight _____

13 I want to make positive changes in my life _____

14 I will confront my eating disorder voice _____

15 My friends will be supportive of my recovery _____

16 I have more self-acceptance of my body _____

17 I understand that I will need to be in long-term outpatient therapy _____

List your top five recovery goals in order of importance and give plans for achieving these goals

Example goal *Never purge again*

Plans to achieve this goal

1 Follow my menu plan so I am not tempted to purge

2 Try to understand what is stressing me and making me feel anxious

3 Enlist family and friends to give me support and keep me accountable. (if I do purge, I will be honest to myself and others so they can give me more support)

4 Use my coping skills to deal with the urge to purge

5 Remember the medical complications of purging behaviors

First goal

Plans to achieve this goal

1

2

3

4

5

Second goal

Plans to achieve this goal

1

2

3

4

5

Third goal

Plans to achieve this goal

1

2

3

4

5

Fourth goal

Plans to achieve this goal

1

2

3

4

5

Fifth goal

Plans to achieve this goal

1

2

3

4

5

Draw a picture of your body as you feel about it today

How do you want your family or friends to help you with meal preparation/monitoring, therapy, or any other problem areas, such as school or work?

1

2

3

4

5

6

7

8

9

10

List and make plans for activities that you look forward to

Example:
Activity: I want to return to competitive swimming
Plan: Have my therapist or MD talk to my coach about my eating disorder. I will maintain my healthy weight. If I lose weight, I will not be able to practice or compete.

1 Activity:

   Plan:

2 Activity:

   Plan:

3 Activity:

   Plan:

4 Activity:

   Plan:

Intuition

Intuition is the ability to sense the implications of one's choices. Intuition is generally the first answer that comes to mind. When a person faces a decision, intuition tells them whether the path feels positive (harmonious and peaceful) or negative (anxiety-filled and conflicted).

Therapists will ask patients: "What does your intuition tell you about this decision that you are about to make? Imagine standing at a fork in the road and having to decide which path feels better." Patients often answer: "I do not feel anything." They should then ask themselves: *Will this decision or action hurt someone, including me?* A positive path is usually the one in which no one is hurt. Sometimes decisions cannot be made right away because more information is needed. Often, the right decision will become more obvious over time.

Fear can cloud the intuitive path. Like the voice of fear, the eating disorder voice prevents a person from hearing their intuition. When confused by a choice, a person can ask: *What am I afraid of? What would I do if I were not afraid?* A positive path may then become more evident.

A person will know when they are on a negative path because they feel insecure and have little to no confidence in their decision-making abilities. Nothing seems to go right. Everything seems forced. Everything is a fight. A bad decision can haunt a person, whereas a good decision feels right and leaves the person at peace with themselves.

On a negative path, time becomes a punishment. The present is something to be escaped, and every past decision is second-guessed. A person heading down the wrong path spends a lot of time envisioning a "better" situation. A person on a positive path values their time and feels confident about their decisions.

Patients should not lie to themselves about positive paths and negative paths. Justification of a negative path can cause a patient to feel even more confused and lost. Realizing that one is on a negative path leads to clarity, which then allows a patient to change paths.

Lindsay's example

Lindsay has bulimia nervosa. She began purging because the popular girls at school purge together after eating lunch. Lindsay feels uneasy about her decision to purge but was afraid that if she did not participate, she would lose friends. When Lindsay began purging at home after dinner, her parents became suspicious and confronted her. She lied and denied any purging behavior. Lindsay knows that she is heading down a negative path and must not lie to herself or she will lose the ability to find a positive path.

Every choice can either be a step towards wellness or a step towards insecurity and fear. If one can intuitively sense the difference between a positive and a negative path, then they are able to develop higher self-esteem and self-confidence.

When you reach the end of what you should know,
you will be at the beginning of what you should sense.

Kahlil Gibran

List positive paths that you have experienced

1

2

3

List negative paths that you have experienced

1

2

3

Perseverance

Perseverance is the persistence towards a goal despite opposition or discouragement. Life is full of obstacles and hindrances. By persevering through obstacles, a person gains the wisdom and confidence to manage the world around them.

Helen Keller, who became blind and deaf from illness at the age of two, said:

> Impatient with frustrations, we ask ourselves why terrible obstacles should be placed in our path. We cannot but wonder at times why we cannot have smooth sailing instead of being compelled always to fight against adverse winds and rough seas. No doubt the reason is that character cannot be developed in ease and quiet. Only through experiences of trial and suffering can the soul be strengthened, vision cleared, ambition inspired and success achieved.

Perseverance is something that is learned and tested in the classroom, on the sports field, and in the home. Persevering in recovery means that a patient with AN stays honest with themselves about how much they have eaten during the day. If they have restricted a meal or snack, they will replace the food later in the day or at night, thus ensuring that they have eaten the appropriate amount of food for the day.

An eating disorder is an opportunistic illness. When life becomes difficult with work, school, or family, the eating disorder voice becomes louder. Perseverance in recovery enables a patient to confront the voice that urges them to purge, to lose five pounds, or to lie to themselves.

The Ladder of St. Augustine
Henry Wadsworth Longfellow

The heights by great men reached and kept
Were not attained by sudden flight,
But they, while their companions slept,
Were toiling upward in the night.

What advice would you give to other patients with an eating disorder?

1

2

3

4

5

Write a letter saying goodbye to your eating disorder

Draw a picture or write a paragraph of the life you want in one year

Draw a picture or write a paragraph of the life you want in five years

What is recovery?

I will maintain a healthy weight.

I have self-acceptance of my body.

I will resist cultural influences to be thin.

I will maintain my weight through healthy eating and appropriate exercise.

I will eat meals without exhibiting eating disorder behaviors.

I will treat myself to my favorite foods without feeling guilty or binge eating.

I will learn to eat when I am hungry and stop when I am full.

I have learned positive coping skills for stress, anger, and depression.

I have learned to express my thoughts and feelings appropriately.

I have learned positive coping skills to deal with urges to restrict or have binge-eating/purging behaviors.

I will continue to be honest with myself and others.

I will continue to gain self-esteem and self-confidence.

I will forgive myself and others.

I appreciate my many positive traits.

I enjoy my own sense of individuality.

I will confront fear with courage and will keep a positive attitude about life's lessons.

I have improved my relationships with my family.

I have reconnected with positive friends.

I have become involved in activities that I enjoy.

I am able to return to school, work, or volunteer activities.

Signs of relapse

1   I focus on my weight.

2   I think about restricting food to lose just five pounds.

3   I start coping with stress and other emotions by restricting my eating.

4   I constantly think about food and calories.

5   I stop telling my therapist the truth about my food intake.

7   I skip my weigh-in appointments with the physician.

8   I water load before weigh-in appointments.

9   I constantly read food labels.

10 I buy and eat low fat and low calorie foods.

11 I have started using diet pills, laxatives, or diuretics.

12 I worry about every piece of food that goes into my body.

13 I return to my compulsive behaviors around food.

14 I eat slowly and cut food into small pieces.

15 I eat excessively fast.

16 I begin to bake and cook often for others.

17 I no longer follow my meal plan.

18 I skip meals.

19 I begin to secretly purge after meals.

20 I do subtle forms of exercise to burn calories.

21 I excessively exercise or run even when my body hurts.

22 I begin to think that if I am thinner, I will feel better about myself.

23 I hear a compliment about my looks and automatically assume that I am fat.

24 I see a model in a magazine and want to achieve their thinness.

25 I begin to feel guilty about my eating disorder behaviors.

26 I withdraw from friends because I don't want them to see how much I am eating.

27 I start coping with stress and other emotions by having binge-eating/purging episodes.

28 I can only hear my eating disorder voice.

29 I start measuring and weighting my food.

30 I am irritable and anxious most of the time.

"The first step towards relapse is a lie."

Lenore McKnight

Discharge

1 A patient with AN has reached their healthy weight as determined by the treatment team.

2 A patient has stable vital signs.

3 A patient has been eating 100 % of their meal plans without exhibiting eating disorder behaviors.

4 A patient with BN is no longer having episodes of restricting food or having binge-eating/ purging behaviors, such as self-induced vomiting, inappropriate use of medications, or excessive exercising.

5 A patient will participate in healthy exercise as recommended by the treatment team.

6 A patient has been participating in all therapy groups.

7 A patient has shown good insight into the causes of their eating disorder.

8 A patient has positive coping skills to deal with eating disorder thoughts and behaviors that may arise.

9 A patient has self-acceptance of their body and has an appreciation for their positive traits.

10 A patient has learned to express their feelings appropriately.

11 A patient has reconnected with family and friends.

12 A patient feels confident about returning to school, work, or volunteer activities.

DISCHARGE
SIGN-OFF

THERAPIST _____

DIETITIAN (RD) _____

PHYSICIAN (MD) _____

Bibliography

American Psychiatric Association. 2013. *Diagnostic and Statistical Manual of Mental Disorders,* 5th Edition: DSM-5. Arlington, VA: American Psychiatric Association.

American Psychiatric Association. 2006. *Practice Guidelines for the Treatment of Patients with Eating Disorders,* 3rd ed. Arlington, VA: American Psychiatric Association.

Arcelus J, Mitchell AJ, Wales J, and Nielsen S. 2011. Mortality rates in patients with anorexia nervosa and other eating disorders: A meta-analysis of 36 studies. *Archives of General Psychiatry* 68:724-731.

Clark, J. 1989. *The Human Body: A Comprehensive Guide to the Structures and Functions of the Human Body.* New York: Arch Cape Press.

Curie, M. 2017. Retrieved October 12, 2017 from http://www.goodreads.com/author/quotes/126903.Marie_Curie.

Douglas, A. 2016. *2412 Mark Twain Quotes.* Amazon Digital Services LLC.

Duytt, R. 2017. *Academy of Nutrition and Dietetics Complete Food and Nutrition Guide*, 5th Edition. New York: Muffin Harcourt Publishing Company.

Eddy KT, Tabri N, Thomas JJ, Murry H, Keshaviah A, Hastings E,... Franco, D. 2017. Recovery from anorexia nervosa and bulimia nervosa at 22-year follow-up. *The Journal of Clinical Psychiatry* 78:184-189.

Fichter MM, Quadflieg N, Crosby RD, and Koch C. 2017. Long-term outcome of anorexia nervosa: Results from a large clinical longitudinal study. *International Journal of Eating Disorders* 50:1018-1030.

Gibran, K. 1965. *Sand and Foam.* New York: Alfred A. Knopf.

EATING DISORDERS

Grilo, C. and James, M. 2010. *The Treatment of Eating Disorders: A Clinical Handbook*. New York: Guilford Press.

Henley, W. 1958. "Invictus." In Roy J. Cook, ed., *101 Famous Poems*. New York: McGraw-Hill.

Herzog D, Dorer DJ, Keel PK, Selwyn SE, Ekeblad ER, Flores AT, Greenwood DN, Burwell RA, and Keller MB. 1999. Recovery and relapse in anorexia and bulimia nervosa: A 7.5 year follow-up study. *Journal of the American Academy of Child and Adolescent Psychiatry* 38:829-837.

Igra, V. 2000, April 10. "Medical Complications of Eating Disorders." Presented at the Kaiser Eating Disorders Conference. Oakland.

Kaye WH, Fudge JL, and Paulus M. 2009. New Insights into symptoms and neurocircuit function of anorexia nervosa. *Nature Review Neuroscience* 10:255-260.

Keller, H. 1967. In Jack Belck, ed. T*he Faith of Helen Keller: the Life of a Great Woman, with Selections from Her Writings*. Kansas City: Hallmark Cards.

Kouba S, Hailstrom T, Lindholm C, and Hirschberg AL. 2005. Pregancy and neonatal outcomes in women with eating disorders. *Obstetrics and Gynecology* 105:255-260.

Lawson E, Donoho D, Miller KK, Misra M, Meenaghan E, Lydecker J, Wexler T, Herzog DB, and Klibanski A. 2009. Hypercortisolemia is Associated with Severity of Bone Loss and Depression in Hypothalamic Amenorrhea in Anorexia Nervosa. *Journal of Clinical Endocrinology and Metabolism* 94:4710-4716.

Longfellow, H. 1992. "The Ladder of St. Augustine." *Favorite Poems, Dover Thrift Editions*. New York: Dover Publications, Inc.

Longfellow, H. 1839. *Hyperion*, Book III. Chapter IV.

Markhamm, E. 2015. " A Creed to Mr. David Lubin." *Lincoln and Other Poems*. London: Forgotten Books.

Mehler P. and Andersen A. 2017. *Eating Disorders A Guide to Medical Care and Complications,* 3rd Edition. Baltimore: The John Hopkins University Press.

Mehler P. and Frank G. 2016. Special Issue, Medical Complications of Eating Disorders. *International Journal of Eating Disorders* 49;216-344.

Micali N, Simonoff E, and Treasure J. 2011. Pregnancy and postpartum depression and anxiety in a longitudinal general population cohort: The effect of eating disorders and past depression. *Journal of Affective Disorders* 131:150-157.

NIH. 2017. *The Digestive System:* http://www.niddk.nih.gov/health-information/digestive-diseases/digestive-system-how-it-works.

Norton, J. 2000 June. *Clinical Correlates of Anorexia Nervosa in Adolescent Inpatient Populations.* Presented to the Faculty of John F. Kennedy University Graduate School of Professional Psychology. (Permission given for this information via email.)

Pasternak Y, Weintraub AY, Shoham-Vardi I, ed al. 2012. Obstetric and perinatal outcome in women with eating disorders. *Journal of Women's Health 26:61-65.*

Samelson, D. 2009. *Feeding the Starving Mind A Personalized, Comprehensive Approach to Overcoming Anorexia and Other Starvation Eating Disorders.* Oakland: New Harbinger Publications, Inc.

Shakespeare, W. 2001. *All's Well that Ends Well.* New York: Simon and Schuster Paperbacks.

Shaw, N. 1999. *Mistakes and Missteps in Working with Eating Disorder Patients and Strategies for Clinicians to Manage Them.* Oakland: Self-published.

Steinhausen, H. 2002. The outcome of anorexia nervosa in the 20th Century. *American Journal of Psychiatry* 159:1284-1293.

Titove OE, Hjorth OC, Schioth HB, and Brooks SJ. 2013. Anorexia Nervosa is linked to reduced brain structure in reward and somatosensory regions: A meta-analysis of VBM studies. *BMC Psychiatry* 13:110-114.

About the Author

Lenore McKnight earned her medical degree from the University of California San Francisco Medical School, completing her adult psychiatry residency and child psychiatry fellowship at Langley Porter Psychiatric Institute, UCSF. She is board certified in adult psychiatry as well as in child and adolescent psychiatry. After working in private outpatient practice in Northern California for more than a decade, Dr. McKnight accepted a position with Kaiser Permanente, where she established an inpatient adolescent eating disorders program at a San Francisco Bay Area hospital. Dr. McKnight is now retired after spending twenty-two years treating Kaiser inpatients and PHP patients with eating disorders.

Made in the USA
Monee, IL
18 June 2024

60051191R00096